More Praise for *Culture Crossing*

"The most powerful influence on attitude and behavior is one's culture—and this book shows you how to be more effective with more people from different cultures."
—**Brian Tracy, author of *How the Best Leaders Lead***

"I wish I had this book sooner! Between working abroad in India and starting a company in New York City, I've found myself in so many situations where I didn't know what the cultural norm was, and I know this book would have helped me adjust to otherwise unfamiliar situations much more quickly. I can't wait to apply the lessons I've learned from *Culture Crossing* to situations I know I'll find myself in in the future."
—**Liz Wessel, cofounder and CEO, WayUp**

"Michael combines a rare and deep understanding of global cultural issues with humor to create awareness on one of the most important topics of our era. His stories and teachings have been invaluable for us at SAP Academy, as we have trained hundreds of millennials from over fifty countries in our global training facility. If you serve in any organization or role in which you work with people from different cultures, *run*, don't walk, to read this book."
—**Rae Kyriazis, Global Vice President, SAP**

"Understanding culture is the key to creating and maintaining successful relationships in this increasingly global world. This book is a must-read for those just entering the workforce to the leaders of top companies."
—**Alex Churchill, Executive Chairman, VonChurch, and CEO, Gamesmith**

"Drawing upon his own extensive international experience, Michael has created an indispensable tool for anyone who interacts with people from other cultures. (And who among us doesn't?) Michael's insights, told in an easy-to-follow style and illustrated with eye-opening anecdotes, will help so many global citizens open up their minds and better understand each other—more easily accomplishing their mutual objectives."
—**Luciana Duarte, Global Head of Employee Communications, Engagement, and Culture, HP Inc.**

"The most profound reality we face as marketers is the multicultural fractionalization of our marketplace. We are perplexed by this, so we continue to talk in our own voice rather than learning how to listen to these diverse voices with an empathy that is agile and truly customer-centric. Michael Landers has changed the way our people think and act with his method and teaching."
—**Bill McDonough, Senior Vice President and Chief Marketing Office, M/I Homes**

Culture Crossing

CULTURE CROSSING

Discover the Key to Making Successful
Connections in the New Global Era

MICHAEL LANDERS

BK

Berrett–Koehler Publishers, Inc.
a BK Business book

BERRETT-KOEHLER PUBLISHERS, INC.
1333 Broadway, Suite 1000, Oakland, CA 94612-1921
Tel: (510) 817-2277   Fax: (510) 817-2278   www.bkconnection.com

ORDERING INFORMATION

QUANTITY SALES. Special discounts are available on quantity purchases by corporations, associations, and others. For details, contact the "Special Sales Department" at the Berrett-Koehler address above.

INDIVIDUAL SALES. Berrett-Koehler publications are available through most bookstores. They can also be ordered directly from Berrett-Koehler:
Tel: (800) 929-2929; Fax: (802) 864-7626; www.bkconnection.com

ORDERS FOR COLLEGE TEXTBOOK/COURSE ADOPTION USE. Please contact Berrett-Koehler: Tel: (800) 929-2929; Fax: (802) 864-7626.

Orders by U.S. trade bookstores and wholesalers. Please contact Ingram Publisher Services, Tel: (800) 509-4887; Fax: (800) 838-1149; E-mail: customer.service@ingrampublisherservices.com; or visit www.ingrampublisherservices.com/Ordering for details about electronic ordering.

Berrett-Koehler and the BK logo are registered trademarks of Berrett-Koehler Publishers, Inc.

Printed in Canada

Berrett-Koehler books are printed on long-lasting acid-free paper. When it is available, we choose paper that has been manufactured by environmentally responsible processes. These may include using trees grown in sustainable forests, incorporating recycled paper, minimizing chlorine in bleaching, or recycling the energy produced at the paper mill.

LIBRARY OF CONGRESS CATALOGING-IN-PUBLICATION DATA

Names: Landers, Michael, 1971– author.
Title: Culture crossing : discover the key to making successful connections in the new global era / Michael Landers.
Description: Oakland : Berrett-Koehler Publishers, [2016]
Identifiers: LCCN 2016038080 | ISBN 9781626567108 (pbk.)
Subjects: LCSH: Cultural competence. | Intercultural communication. | Organizational behavior—Cross-cultural studies.
Classification: LCC HM793 .L36 2016 | DDC 303.48/2—dc23
LC record available at https://lccn.loc.gov/2016038080

First Edition

21 20 19 18 17 16   10 9 8 7 6 5 4 3 2 1

Cover design: Ian Koviak, The Book Designers. Book production and interior design: VJB/Scribe.
Copyeditor: Kristi Hein. Proofreader: Nancy Bell. Indexer: Rae Rice

For Talia Belle: May your life be filled with cultural adventures, in a world filled with peace and understanding.

Know thyself.

—SOCRATES

| CONTENTS

CONCLUSION

Culture Crossings Past, Present, and Future 171

Culture Crashing

We are all just one step away from a culture crash—a phenomenon that occurs when someone from one culture unintentionally confuses, frustrates, or offends a person from another culture.

Why are we in danger of culture crashing, and more importantly, why should we care?

In this global era, when people, money, and information are flowing faster than ever across international borders, more and more of the individuals with whom you interact are from other cultures. If you don't learn how to avoid or recover from a culture crash, you will undoubtedly miss out on opportunities to build better connections and achieve greater success in all your business and personal endeavors. In this book I offer the key to truly thriving in this new global era—a skill set that will empower you to seize opportunities and create more peaceful and prosperous culture crossings in the diverse arenas where we work and live.

Culture crashes have long made headlines, as in 2013, when Microsoft founder Bill Gates insulted the South Korean president by keeping one hand in his pocket while shaking her hand[1]—or in 2016, when Argentinian soccer player Lionel Messi offended an entire nation by donating his used shoes to raise money for an Egyptian charity.[2] Apparently no one told Messi that shoes are considered dirty and lowly in Egyptian culture—the ultimate symbol of disrespect.

Of course, international business mavens and sports stars aren't the only ones prone to culture crashing. With more than 244 million people currently living outside their country of origin,[3] it's little wonder that these crashes are becoming more frequent and the consequences more problematic for all of us—although we often don't even realize that *culture is the culprit*. Think about your own interactions. Have you ever written someone off as disrespectful or shifty because he didn't look you in the eye? Has a salesperson's communication style ever stopped you from buying something you wanted? Has someone's way of negotiating or getting to know you ever felt overly aggressive? How about feeling annoyed because your boss didn't credit you for your accomplishments at work or the feedback you received from a colleague seemed totally inappropriate? While many of us have had experiences like these, we rarely stop to contemplate whether the person's behavior was culturally motivated—or how our own cultural programming could have caused us to completely misinterpret what we observed.

It used to be that culture crashes occurred mostly when we traveled abroad—such problems arose "over there." Today, crashes are just as likely to occur on our home turf, where our communities and workplaces are diversifying at an astonishing rate. It's a trend that's reflected in countries and cities around the globe. The United States, for example, is home to more than 42 million documented immigrants,[4] more than four times as many as in 1970.[5]

By 2065, immigrants are projected to account for 88 percent of the population increase in the United States, or 103 million people, as the nation grows to 441 million.[6] In the state of California alone one in four people is an immigrant, and there are thirty-five recognized nationalities, speaking more than fifty-five languages.[7]

The changing makeup of California's population is not exceptional. Consider some examples. The percentage of foreign-born people living in Miami is 38.5.[8] Dearborn, Michigan, boasts the largest proportion of Arab Americans of any U.S. city,[9] and the Washington, DC metropolitan area is home to a thriving community of tens of thousands of Ethiopians. The U.S. heartland is going global too, thanks in part to an influx of international students. College towns like

Tuscaloosa, Alabama, and Lincoln, Nebraska, are flooded with foreign students from all corners of the world, with the largest and fastest-growing percentage coming from China. In the college town of Iowa City, Iowa, bubble tea shops (selling a Taiwanese tea drink filled with tiny chewy balls) now outnumber Starbucks three to one, and nearly one in ten students at the University of Iowa hails from China.[10]

A major rise in the number of students moving across borders in pursuit of higher education also contributes to increased diversity in our communities. Twenty years ago, some 42,500 students from China attended a college or university in the United States. In 2015, that number reached nearly 275,000, with most coming for undergraduate degrees.[11] This diversification of our schools and communities brings opportunities for cultural enrichment, but it also brings the inevitability of miscommunications, no matter how fluently someone seems to speak your language.

On the business front, these students—and the hundreds of thousands of others who will continue to settle in the United States in the coming decades[12]—represent an astounding wave of new consumer potential. Consumer potential is also exploding on other business fronts—including virtual ones, thanks to ever-improving communication technologies and the diversifying global economy. In the coming years, new players will make and expand their mark—countries like Vietnam, India, China, Saudi Arabia, and Nigeria, whose economies are predicted to grow between 6 and 9 percent a year over the next thirty years (Germany and the United States, on the other hand, are expected to grow only 2 to 3 percent per year).[13] Until recently, most of the world's middle class—with all of its buying power and potential—resided in Europe and North America. But the middle class in the Asia Pacific region is projected to surge from its current 18 percent to 66 percent by 2025.[14]

The cultural diversification of our national and global marketplaces is a game changer. Tried and true strategies for doing business are no longer working, because of cultural differences related to everything from what motivates buyers, to the way we negotiate, to how we interpret a gesture. The unintended consequences of our cultural obliviousness include conflicts, missed opportunities, and the loss of money, credibility, and trust—inhibiting our ability to build deeper and more trusting relationships with colleagues, clients, and customers.

Try as we might to educate ourselves, it is impossible to know the customs, nuances, and hot buttons of every culture with which we come in contact. And while there are books about what to do and not do when interacting with people from certain cultures, the advice they offer tends to be too specific or superficial to truly offer any benefit in an era in which multiculturalism is fast becoming the new norm.

Fortunately, there is a better and more personally enriching way to navigate culture crossings with savvy and success. It's a method that depends on your willingness to look inward; to unpack your own cultural baggage and learn how to get control over your cultural reflexes.

Culture is an aspect of our psychology that we often overlook. Although some of our behaviors are attributable to influences like personality traits and individual experiences, many of our communication styles, perceptions, and expectations are also the result of deep-rooted cultural conditioning. Like any other habitual behavior, our cultural habits are hard to break—right up there with coffee and cigarettes. Culture has blazed neural pathways in our brains that trigger automatic responses over which we exert little control.

In this book I offer a proven method for uncovering and gaining control of your own cultural programming, which in turn will enable you to significantly improve your cross-cultural agility. Like anything worth doing, it takes some time and practice, but it is wholly achievable and increasingly vital to your success in this global era. Through a mix of stories, insights, and self-investigation exercises you'll acquire a basic but essential understanding of many ways that we are all influenced by culture, which will enable you to enhance your interactions with people from all cultures, professions, and walks of life. I've successfully used this approach over the past two decades to help individuals from Fortune 500 companies, non-profit organizations, educational institutions, and many other kinds of communities around the globe to build stronger and more profitable relationships across cultures. It's a methodology that I actually began developing when I was fairly young, as a means of preserving my own sanity.

Although I was born in the United States, I spent fifteen of my grade school years in Latin America. I attended three high schools over the course of four years in three different countries—an experience that forced me to endure repeated bouts of culture shock. Every summer after school ended, I returned to the United States and hung around with kids who didn't know where countries like Brazil and Colombia were on the map. They would ask me how I got to school in these exotic places, and I would answer by telling them with a straight face that "we swung from vines," as their eyes widened in disbelief.

Of course, to get to school in those countries I took a bus or rode in a car, and I spent my days doing the same things that they did. But there *were* some differences. By the time I was a teenager, I realized that it wasn't just that my U.S. friends couldn't relate to many of my experiences (and didn't really care to); our interactions were often puzzling to each other. We had different expectations and actions related to everything from greeting etiquette, to the value we placed on time, to how we dated. It made me hyperaware of my own cultural programming and adept at adjusting my behaviors so that I wouldn't be teased for my "foreign" ways.

It was these early experiences that charted the course for my career, leading me to earn a master's in cross-cultural studies and establish my own consulting firm. Those early years and my later studies instilled in me a deep passion for exploring other cultures. My work enables me to continually expand my knowledge and deepen my understanding of different cultures, and consequently of my own. The insights I share with you in this book are the same ones that have enabled me to see myself and others more clearly, and to move through the world in a more mindful way. My hope is that in reading this book, you too will enjoy the process of becoming more culturally mindful and laying the foundation for your own personal success in the new global era.

Got Culture?

Before you read any further, let's make sure we are on the same page about the meaning of *culture* as it pertains to this book. Look at any online dictionary and you'll find several meanings. One relates to "the arts and other manifestations of human intellectual achievement regarded collectively." There are also the more biologically associated meanings, including "the growing of plants or breeding of particular animals in order to get a particular substance or crop from them," and "a group of cells or bacteria grown for medical or scientific study." The meaning of culture that we employ in this book does in fact have to do with the process of cultivating something, but is thankfully free of microbes and mold spores:

> culture [noun]
> The customs and beliefs, art, way of life and social organization of a particular country or group.

This vast definition of culture includes tangible behaviors such as eating, dress, language, customs, and traditions as well as intangibles such as beliefs, values, assumptions, expectations, and attitudes. Collectively cultivated and reinforced by a group over time, these factors combine to create the basis for cultural identity. They dictate how we interact with each other and with our environments.

Culture isn't restricted to people's ethnic, national, or regional identities. Companies, organizations, schools, summer camps, families, and other groups have their own cultures too. Cultural traits can also differ between genders and across economic lines. This definition of culture isn't even unique to humans. Studies of primates, cetaceans (like whales and dolphins), birds, and other animal communities have shown that these species cultivate cultures of their own.[15] What *is* unique to humans is the complexity of the cultural webs that envelop and influence us and that define our lives.

Our cultural identities are a mash-up of all of those groups with which we associate. That said, I've chosen to focus largely on national and ethnic cultures because of their formative and often sustaining impact on our beliefs, values, and behaviors. Engrained from an early age (starting in the third trimester in the womb, when we begin to hear language[16]), people almost always unconsciously bring the influence of their national and ethnic cultures to the table when they get involved with smaller subgroups. I've also chosen to focus on national and ethnic cultures because they have been studied and documented so extensively, providing us with a credible platform from which to explore, compare, and contrast tendencies.

Nevertheless, the lessons offered in this book are applicable when it comes to improving your interactions within any kind of culture, and they offer surprising insights about the way we as individuals perceive the world. In the following chapters, you may discover things about yourself and your culture that you never knew or fully acknowledged. I hope you will develop a deeper understanding of how we are all impacted by culture in profound ways. You hold in your hands the key to creating your own personal road map for successfully navigating today's multicultural communities and marketplaces, and to cultivating a new kind of self-awareness that will serve you in all facets of your life.

ONE

Cultural Awakenings

How culture shapes our thoughts and behaviors

When you ask a five-year-old kid from the United States what a dog says, he or she will probably say "woof-woof" or "bow-wow." Ask a kid living in Japan, and you're likely to get a "wan-wan." Try it in Iran, and you'll hear "hauv-hauv." In Laos they say "voon-voon." It's "gong-gong" in Indonesia and "mung-mung" in Korea.

Besides being a fun bit of knowledge to share at a dinner party, animal sounds are a good example of how people from different cultures are programmed from an early age to interpret the same experiences in different ways. It also underscores how culturally specific perceptions can get deeply lodged in our brains. Imagine if you suddenly had to convince yourself that your dog was saying "voon-voon." Unless you are from Laos, it would probably take a while.

Here's another example: think about how you indicate yes and no without using words. For most people in the United States, the answer is simple: nodding your head up and down means "yes," and turning your head left and right means "no." In Bulgaria, however, nodding your head up and down means "no," and turning your head left and right means "yes"!

Just for fun, here's a challenge for you, to test your own programming: try answering the following two questions with a nonverbal "yes" or "no," but do it the Bulgarian way, turning your head side to side for "yes," and up and down for "no."

Do you want to win the lottery?

Would you pay $100 for a hamburger?

For most people, answering these questions is probably more challenging than you expected it to be. After hearing, seeing, believing, or doing anything a particular way throughout your whole life, it can be extremely difficult to change the way you act, react, or perceive someone else's behaviors. It's all a result of programming, some of which is biologically hardwired and some of which is based on our experiences. Your cultural programming comprises various combinations of values, perceptions, attitudes, beliefs, assumptions, expectations, and behaviors—and it plays a large role in shaping our identities, providing us with instructions for how to navigate our lives.

In our earliest years we're taught things like language, manners, societal do's and don'ts, punishable behaviors, and what sound a dog makes. As our cultural programming continues to accrue and be reinforced over our lifetimes, it manifests in the way we make decisions, problem solve, perceive time, build trust, communicate, buy and sell, and even how we die.

Some of our cultural programming has been handed down to us by ancestors who lived thousands of years ago, but our programming is also continuously rewritten by contemporary communities, seeking to make sense of outdated programming in a modern context. We as individuals have the choice to adapt our personal programming to new scenarios and surroundings, or not. It's the technological equivalent of updating your operating system. If you don't perform the update, your functionality may be compromised.

Despite the profound ways in which culture influences our personas, most of us are barely aware of it—that is, until we encounter people whose cultural programming is different from ours. Our minds—

our personal operating systems—may freeze up and crash just as our electronic devices do. Instead of manifesting as a frozen screen, it causes us to feel uncomfortable, perplexed, and frustrated. We may shut down, explode with emotion, or simply give up and walk away—thereby missing out on opportunities to build positive relations and achieve success at work and in other aspects of our lives. I call these kinds of encounters *culture crashes*.

When culture crashes happen, it is often a result of *unconscious incompetence*. More simply put: "You don't know what you don't know." Acknowledging that you are in the dark is actually the first step to increasing your self-awareness and avoiding the kind of "crash" just described. It means you are ready to open your mind to things you may never have considered before.

Some of our behaviors are modeled on those we have seen or heard, like how to make animal noises or indicate yes or no. But there are hundreds, if not thousands of other more nuanced behaviors whose cultural origins are less apparent. These are things like how close you usually stand to a friend or colleague while talking, how promptly you show up for a party or business function, or whether and when you look someone in the eye.

While some of these habits can be chalked up to individual personality or experience, many of them are rooted in culture. For example, when I ask people from the United States what makes someone seem trustworthy to them, one of the most common answers is: "Someone who looks me directly in the eye." So when someone doesn't look them in the eye, they immediately begin to question whether or not this person is trustworthy.

In many Western cultures, direct eye contact is viewed as a sign of respect and expected between people of all ages and genders. But in parts of Thailand, Oman, and Japan, direct eye contact is often construed as a sign of disrespect, especially between genders and people of different ages.

I can clearly remember my first experience with eye contact

confusion when I moved to Japan to teach English in my early twenties. I was struck by how practically none of my students would look me in the eye, even those who were significantly older than I was. In the United States, this would have been construed as a sign of disrespect, but in Japan, avoiding eye contact with your teachers is a show of deference. I tried to train my students to look me in the eye when speaking English, and they eventually got the hang of it. Meanwhile, I was busy trying to retrain myself to avoid the eyes of my Japanese martial arts master. It was much more challenging than I anticipated.

The way we greet others is also something we are culturally programmed to do at a very young age, but the way in which we perform these greetings is continually refined over time as we learn about the more subtle implications. Consider all of the nuances of a gesture as seemingly simple as a handshake. The strength and length of your grasp, the hand you use, and what you do with your eyes while you shake all have certain implications. In the United States, a firm handshake generally signifies a sense of confidence—a positive attribute. Conversely, offering a limp, "dead fish" handshake can cause the person on the receiving end of the shake to feel uncomfortable and question the confidence, authenticity, and professionalism of the other person. If the handshake is firm but lingers too long and turns into a handhold, people may feel uncomfortable or threatened by behavior interpreted as pushy, and they may start to question the person's motives.

Meanwhile, in parts of the Middle East and Africa, the same lingering handshake often signifies respect, admiration, or commitment to the personal or business relationship. If someone tries to pull away too quickly, it could be viewed as a sign of disrespect or lack of trust and dedication.

Former President George W. Bush was well coached in 2005 when he strolled through the garden of his Crawford, Texas, compound holding hands with Crown Prince Abdullah of Saudi Arabia, in an effort to improve relations and lower oil prices.[1] But photos and videos of them holding hands struck a nerve with U.S. citizens. It became fodder for news reporters and late night talk show hosts, and "man on the street" interviews in U.S. cities revealed how people were agitated by the handholding and struggled to make sense of its implications.[2]

Now consider how someone might not be aware of any or all of these nuances if he or she was raised in a culture where handshaking is not a typical greeting. If you had grown up in a place like Korea or Japan you probably would have been taught to bow as a greeting, and learned to do it to the correct depth, depending on the person or the context. In Thailand you might be assessed for the position of your *wai*, a common greeting that entails holding your palms pressed together and held close to your chest while slowly lowering your head. In places like Italy, Lebanon, and Brazil, you would learn to dole out the appropriate number of kisses and exactly where and how firmly to plant them on someone's cheek.

The nuances of all these gestures are equally as subtle as those for the U.S. handshake. Of course, behaviors like greetings and eye contact are just the tip of the iceberg when it comes to differences in our cultural conditioning. Look below the surface, and we start to uncover some of the underlying reasons why we do what we do, and we begin to discover the key to increasing our cross-cultural awareness.

Cultural Icebergs

Boarding a public bus in Colombo, Sri Lanka, can feel at times like trying to be the first one through the doors of Walmart on Black Friday. Or at least that's how it was described to me by a friend who traveled to this tear-shaped island off the coast of southern India a few years ago.

Based on her upbringing in the United States, she has certain expectations about how to board buses—or trains or planes, for that matter. She doesn't always expect people to stand in a perfect line. She's jammed herself into crowded New York City subway cars countless times. But she does assume people will get on a bus in some sort of orderly and courteous fashion. Here in Colombo, however, as they opened the doors at her downtown stop, it was as if a stampede was bearing down on her. Standing in the midst of a crush of bodies trying to squeeze through the narrow doorway was not only startling and illogical to her, but sort of scary too. But mostly she interpreted this behavior as rudeness.

Two things happened during this experience. First, she observed the behavior of the people jamming themselves onto the bus. Second, she interpreted this experience based on how she's been boarding buses her entire life. Her interpretations caused her to feel annoyed, uncomfortable, and disrespected. But what if she didn't have those expectations? What if she had been raised in a culture where everybody boarded a bus this way?

How people stand in line is one of those culturally influenced behaviors that are easy to observe, although we may not even realize that culture is at work behind the scenes. The list of easy-to-spot behaviors includes what people eat, how they dress, the language they speak, the tone of voice they use, gestures, and so on. What's more difficult to observe is the *why* behind these behaviors. And knowing the *why*—or at least being open to the idea that the *whys* can vary significantly—is the first step to improving your cross-cultural agility.

The most obvious answer to the question of why we do what we do is this: because that's what everyone else does. In places like the United States, Great Britain, or Germany, you quickly learn to line up for the bus, and that cutting the line isn't cool. In many parts of China or India, on the other hand, lining up is not generally expected, and people learn quickly that if they don't forge ahead, they may never get on the bus.

But the reason *why* entire groups of people tend to board buses in different ways has to do with the values, beliefs, and attitudes of each culture. In cultures where order and efficiency are highly valued in all aspects of life, these virtues dictate the way people queue up. In other cultures, order is generally viewed as a behavior warranted only in certain situations, not in all facets of life. Another cultural factor that can influence how people line up relates to varying perceptions of space and time—a fascinating subject that we'll explore in chapter five.

By now you've gotten the picture that culture influences us in countless ways, leaving its mark on everything from how we view time and create priorities to how we cultivate relationships and grow old. The building blocks of our cultural programming are values, beliefs, and attitudes—invisible elements that subconsciously drive many of our behaviors.

Invisible is the key word here.

You most likely have seen the iceberg model (Figure 1.1) before in learning and development contexts. I use it here because it can help you wrap your brain around these invisible aspects of your cultural programming.

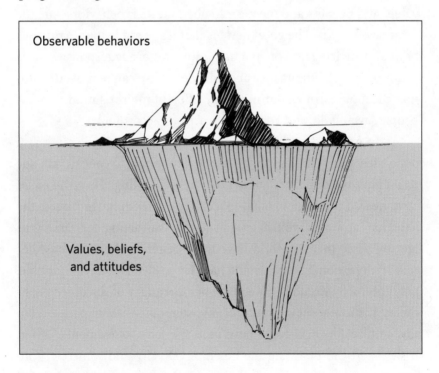

Observable behaviors

Values, beliefs, and attitudes

Figure 1.1: The iceberg

We spend our lives reacting to what we observe—what's above the proverbial waterline. We hear what people say, see what they do, and interpret the nuances of all of this based on our assumptions and prior experiences.

But what if the values, beliefs, and attitudes that lie hidden deep below the waterline are different from our own? Consider that those unseen differences could change the meaning and intent of what someone is saying or doing. What would the implications be?

This is what happened to my friend in Sri Lanka. Her deep-rooted social conditioning caused her to subconsciously assume that everyone else valued public order in the same way that she did. As a result, she interpreted the bus boarding process as chaotic, rude, and disrespectful.

Our minds are hardwired to jump to the conclusion that others' values and beliefs—and the meaning behind their behaviors—are the same as our own. The good news is that it's possible to override our brain's hardwiring and build a new, more culturally responsive navigation system. With practice and knowledge, we can rein in our automatic responses, open our minds to different interpretations of what people say and do, and adjust our reactions accordingly.

As an example, at the Sri Lankan bus stop my friend could have done a few things differently. First, before jumping to conclusions, she could have paused to *recognize* how she was feeling. Then she could have cleared out some mental space to *open her mind* and assess the situation, and observe that everyone else was acting the same way. Having done that, it would have been easier for her to adjust her reflexive reaction. She still would have felt jostled and uncomfortable, but it probably wouldn't have made her feel angry or disrespected, or caused her to start developing negative stereotypes about people from this culture. She also could have used the same assessment method if she had been boarding the bus in a U.S. city and someone from another culture shoved her in order to get on more quickly. Instead of immediately getting upset and lashing out, she could have considered that the person had not yet adapted their own cultural programming to mesh with way people board buses in the United States.

In a similar vein, armed with your new awareness about the nuances of greetings across cultures, you could hit the pause button during a handshake and recognize that any differences from the handshake you expected could be making you jump to false conclusions about the other person. Your heightened awareness might lead you to adjust your own greeting style so you don't make the wrong impression or send an unintended message.

These are just a few examples of the countless scenarios in which improved cultural awareness and adaptability can help you connect with others—as opposed to crashing. In today's globalized communities, workplaces, and markets, raising your level of awareness and adaptability is essential to making successful culture crossings.

Some people might question the need for this kind of cultural dexterity in light of an emerging "global culture"—a sociological phenomenon that suggests cultures are becoming more alike. The rise of this global culture is a result of economic and technological changes that are accelerating and expanding the flow of people and ideas across national boundaries. The ever-broadening dispersal of media, arts, and consumer products is facilitating this diffusion and assimilation of cultural values, preferences, and protocols, changing the way that we behave and think. Global culture is further fostered through advances in communication technology that make it seem easier than ever to communicate and "connect" with people from diverse nationalities. But don't be fooled. There are still plenty of nuances that can and do get lost in translation, largely because it is so difficult to override your earliest and deepest programming. Few if any behaviors are truly universal;[3] no emoji expression will ever be completely fail-safe in its implications.

So how do you retrain your brain to deftly navigate a wide variety of cross-cultural interactions? For starters, you have some unpacking to do.

Unpacking Your Cultural Baggage

Whatever my clients' goals are—whether they are relocating to another country, trying to sell goods and services to recent immigrants on their home turf, or trying to defuse tension in a multicultural office—the first step is always the same: they have to get familiar with the many ways that their own cultural programming influences their behaviors.

Another useful way to wrap your brain around your own programming is to think of it as baggage—*cultural baggage.* Much like *emotional baggage*, cultural baggage is something we unwittingly tote around with us at all times, never knowing when or how it may influence our behaviors.

When we unzip our cultural baggage we can see at a glance those observable behaviors that lie at the top, but not the underlying ideologies that are stuffed deep within or packed away in hidden compartments.

You can start taking inventory of those items in the deepest recesses of your cultural baggage by asking yourself this question: What values truly shape my perceptions, actions, and reactions?

For most of us, it's not an easy question to answer. We often define ourselves by work and lifestyle choices (sales guy, creative type, vegetarian) or by things that we have a passion for (nature, a sports team, food). But we don't spend as much time pondering those core values and beliefs that affect so many of our behaviors—things like individuality, formality, and perceptions of time—largely because in the context of a single culture, it's generally safe to take many of those ideologies for granted. While you may have vast differences of opinion around hot-button political issues, when it comes to certain values, beliefs, and corresponding behaviors, you may find that you are surprisingly in synch with most other people from your culture.

But it can be challenging to identify those core philosophies that unify our own cultures, never mind other cultures. Fortunately, we have at our disposal a good set of investigative tools to jump-start our investigation. We call them proverbs.

Squeaky Wheels and Rolling Stones

One of my favorite parts of delivering cultural training workshops is when I ask people to share a few proverbs from their country or region.

"Hang in there like a hair in a biscuit," was one of the funnier sayings I picked up last year while speaking to a group in Georgia. If you've ever tried to pull a stray hair out of a baked good, you know that this saying is all about tenacity. Although not a quintessential U.S. proverb, this saying clearly speaks to the way that people in the United States value perseverance in many facets of life. Even if someone is unsuccessful—or their efforts are futile—that person is often applauded simply for sticking with it.

The proverbs range from grave to hilarious, but many of them are very telling when it comes to revealing unseen ideologies that drive behaviors in a particular culture. Although some proverbs may be more aspirational than they are actually put into practice, they still offer a useful platform for a first foray into the deep recesses of your cultural baggage.

Consider some other, more classic U.S. proverbs and the messages they send, followed by contrasting proverbs from other cultures.

The squeaky wheel gets the grease. (United States)

From a very early age, most people from the United States are urged to speak up and be heard. Nobody should be silenced. If you don't like your food, tell the chef. If you are being treated unfairly, let someone know. If you don't interrupt and speak up at a meeting, people may think that you didn't add any value.

The proverb "The squeaky wheel gets the grease" is a reflection of the high value that people in the United States place on their constitutional right to openly express themselves and assert their individuality. This freedom was, of course, one of the reasons the first colonists set out for North America.

The duck that quacks the loudest gets shot. (China)

In some countries, asserting your individuality is *not* a driving value. In cultures like Japan, Qatar, and India, group harmony tends to be valued over individuality (something we'll delve into in chapter two). In these cultures, group harmony should not be sacrificed in the name of individual merit or airing differences; hence the Chinese proverb "The duck that quacks the loudest gets shot."

You may have also heard the Japanese proverb "The nail that sticks up gets hammered down," which reflects the same sentiment. While some cultures might interpret this as conformist or oppressive ideology, residents of Japan or China tend to view this as the key to a harmonious community.

If we don't acknowledge or abide by the values illuminated by these proverbs when interacting with people from these cultures, it can become a major obstacle to achieving our goals. When I first began my career in Japan, I attended weekly meetings where the mostly Japanese staff would discuss current issues and goals. One of my responsibilities at this company was marketing, and so I would repeatedly volunteer ideas at these meetings about how the company could reach more customers.

My ideas were always met with head nods in agreement and verbal approvals such as, "Good idea, Michael." But nothing ever happened.

Some six months later I shared my story with a Canadian friend who had been living in Japan for many years, and I discovered that I had been going about it all wrong. He explained that I was supposed to mention my ideas in private to a Japanese peer. Then, if my peer felt the ideas had merit, he or she would share them privately with a more senior peer, who would do the same until it was shared with the manager. All of this would be done in private, behind the scenes.

I decided to give it a try and was shocked when the manager came into the next staff meeting and announced a new marketing plan for the next sales cycle. They were my ideas, presented without any attribution to me. And when the ideas worked and sales increased, there was no reward for me; it was a team win, and that's all that mattered.

God helps those who help themselves. (United States)

People from the United States tend to believe that they are in control of their destiny, and that they can achieve anything to which they set their minds. If you don't like something, you can change it; whether it is your job, your spouse, your nose, or even the natural environment. The proverb "God helps those who help themselves" underscores this notion—as does the expression "Where there's a will, there's a way."

Insha Allah or God willing. (Arab nations)

On the other end of the spectrum are cultures that believe things happen because of the will of God, the universe, or some other higher presence, as opposed to their own will. The expression "*Insha Allah*," translated as "God willing," reflects a belief held widely in Arab countries that our destinies are not in our own hands. The Spanish word *ojala*, which means "hopefully," is actually derived from the Arabic *insha Allah*.

That's not to say that people from Arab countries leave everything up to the will of a more divine power, or that many people in the United States don't believe God's will plays a very important role in determining their future. But there is a tendency within each of these cultures to subscribe to the underlying meaning of the expressions. In other words, some cultures believe that people are mostly in control of the outcomes of our day-to-day actions and decisions, while other cultures continually pay homage to a greater power believed to have a hand in the results of almost everything people do.

When you pose a question to someone from Saudi Arabia such as "So we'll see you tomorrow at the party?" he or she might nod and respond by saying "*Insha Allah*" (God willing). The same expression is used for events that most Westerners would assume require a more definitive answer, such as "Will the supermarket open at 10:00 A.M.?" or "Will you be at the office for the meeting with the new clients at 9:00 tomorrow?" No matter the degree of importance, the answer is often "*Insha Allah*," suggesting a certain level of acceptance that we are not really the masters of our own fate.

You can imagine the pitfalls that await when people with differing perspectives related to who's in control, interact. I've heard many stories from frustrated real estate sellers in the United States about their fruitless attempts to convey a sense of urgency to encourage a sale. "If you don't buy now, prices will go up, " or "This one perfect house will be gone if you don't jump on it" are often successfully used to motivate people from the United States and others to expedite a purchase. But for people who are more of the "God willing" mindset, their attitude is that whether they get the house or not may have little to do with how fast they act. Their thinking may be more along the lines of "It will happen if it's meant to happen." In some cultures, home buyers may be more likely to act swiftly if the address, potential move-in date, or geographic coordinates of the house's location are deemed auspicious by an authority greater than themselves.

Here's another pair of contrasting proverbs from two other countries:

Avoid men who do not speak and dogs that do not bark. (Brazil)

As I can attest from my time living in Brazil, verbal communication is extremely important. As the proverb suggests, Brazilians tend to be more wary of people (or animals) who are relatively quiet than of those who are loquacious and loud. In Brazil, I've found that interrupting during conversations and meetings is common and often expected, and that opinions tend to be offered freely and more frequently compared to many other cultures. These characteristics were highlighted at the 2016 Rio Olympic games, where people from around the globe were struck by the boisterousness of Brazilian fans—especially during events that tend to be more quiet, like ping-pong.[4] The experience was summed up perfectly by this headline from the *Denver Post*: "Boisterous Brazilian fans rewrite rules of Olympic etiquette."[5]

Silence is golden. (Germany)

Although its origin is German, the proverb "Silence is golden" is widely used in parts of Europe as well as North America. The expression underscores the value of silence in certain contexts (but not always), and can suggest that speaking isn't always necessary to acknowledge the moment. It also suggests that some things are better left unsaid. While "Silence is golden" is not the exact opposite of the Brazilian proverb, it does underscore differing perceptions and expectations around the pros and cons of being quiet.

There are also those proverbs that may be used by two different cultures but mean very different things. Take, for example, the U.S. proverb "A rolling stone gathers no moss." This proverb is also used by Japanese, but it means something very different in each culture. In the United States, it suggests that someone should not remain idle; that it's always better to continue moving forward and be active, even if it's not necessarily advancing any particular goal. From the U.S. perspective, the moss symbolizes stagnation and deterioration.

In Japan, however, moss is viewed as a plant that adds beauty and refinement to buildings and gardens as they age. Here, the moss symbolizes the virtues of being patient, and how the value and beauty of something (or someone) can grow with age.

The moss clearly stands for different things in each culture. The differences in the way the proverb is interpreted also underscore differences in cultural ideologies. In Japan, patience is valued as an essential part of the path to success; in the United States, perpetual action is advocated as a way to flourish and succeed.

While age-old proverbs like these do not always reflect the current zeitgeist of a nation or culture, they do point to a set of values embedded in the psyches of earlier generations, many of which have left an indelible mark on the way that people today act and react in various circumstances.

We can't know the values of every culture or person, but by taking stock of proverbs used in our own cultures, we are reminded that there are differing factors that shape perceptions and behaviors in other cultures, and we become less likely to have the kind of negative reactions that stand in the way of building successful connections.

PROVERBS WORTH PONDERING

Consider how these proverbs may reflect cultural beliefs, values, or aspirations.

- A wise man never plays leapfrog with a unicorn. (Tibet)
- A sleeping fox finds no meat. (Brazil)
- Fry the big fish first, the small ones after. (Jamaica)
- A journey of ten thousand steps starts with the first one. (China, Lao Tzu)
- It is good to know the truth, but it is better to speak of palm trees. (Arab nations)
- Truth is like fire; it cannot be hidden under dry leaves. (Africa)
- Stretch your legs as far as your blanket will allow. (Bahrain)
- Sticks in a bundle are unbreakable. (Kenya)

Recognizing Your Reactions

Another good way to identify your own programming is to investigate how you react to specific situations. A simple response to an everyday situation can be revelatory in terms of what you value and what you expect. Try to imagine how you would feel and act in each of the following scenarios. Don't think about it too much; just note your gut reaction to each question, then read the follow-up examples.

You are thirty minutes late to a meeting at work, and everybody on the team is there already. How do you feel? What do you do or say?

For people raised in cultures where punctuality is highly valued, like the United States, we may feel a bit embarrassed by our lateness and offer an apology, along with an excuse to make it clear that it was not our fault. But if you were from a place like Singapore, you may have been taught that interrupting the meeting with an excuse would be construed as a worse offense than being late.

SO WHAT?

As someone from the United States, if you showed up late to a meeting with people from a Singaporean company, your offense would only be made worse by disrupting the meeting with an apology. It would be better to just enter the room and quietly take a seat. But if you are a Singaporean and showed up late to a meeting with someone from the United States and didn't apologize or make an excuse, it would be seen as a sign of disrespect.

You make a statement or pose a question to a colleague and are met with silence. How do you feel? What do you do or say?

Most people from the United States would assume that something is wrong if there's no response after a couple of seconds. Perhaps the person didn't understand or didn't like your statement, or just doesn't know how to answer the question. When awaiting a reply, the silence might begin to make the questioner feel increasingly uncomfortable with each passing moment. In the hyperverbal U.S. culture, silence is often perceived as a symbol of distress.[6]

But in places such as China and Switzerland, the notion of an "awkward silence" is much less prevalent. In these cultures, silence is generally considered socially acceptable and could be imbued with a range of meanings, depending on the context; from avoiding a debate that might disrupt social harmony to simply taking time to contemplate the question and formulate a thoughtful response.

A 2009 study from the University of Ilorin explored how silence is often used as an integral and "communicatively valued piece of 'language'" in Nigeria. Just like spoken words, silence is interpreted in different ways depending on factors such as context and who's participating in the conversation.[7]

SO WHAT?

The default response to prolonged silence in the United States is often to fill the void with noise, forced laughter, or additional questions. If you were to do this with people from cultures in which silence is more acceptable, you would run the risk of interrupting someone's thought process, disrupting the flow and tone of the conversation, and missing out on an opportunity to gain valuable information. In these cultures, unnecessarily filling silence can be associated with immaturity and selfishness, and mark someone as being overly eager.

A guest helps a host carry dirty dishes into the kitchen after a meal. Your thoughts?

This behavior tends to be highly regarded as polite, thoughtful, and humble in many cultures. A host may refuse an offer to help any further with the dishes, but it's always appreciated when guests ask. A guest who doesn't offer can be seen as unappreciative of the hospitality.

However, in some cultures (like Saudi Arabia, Mexico, and Korea) the act of clearing dishes or even offering to help could be construed by the host as disrespectful, possibly suggesting that he or she was doing a poor job.

SO WHAT?

If you are invited to a colleague or customer's house and start clearing the dishes as a show of gratitude, you may actually be insulting the host, whose expectations are different from yours—thereby weakening the relationship and jeopardizing future business deals. On the flip side, if a guest to your home does not offer to help after a meal, don't automatically assume they are being disrespectful or not thankful.

Imagine you are walking down the street and you see someone kick a dog to get him to move out of the way. Your reaction?

Most of the people I know would be outraged. Having grown up with Fido as our best friend, it's hard to imagine why someone would intentionally hurt a dog—including strays. Witnesses might scream bloody murder, accusing the offender of unwarranted cruelty. In a dog-loving culture, kicking a canine is an unthinkable act, sometimes even less acceptable than kicking a family member.

But what if you witnessed this incident in an area where many dogs carry rabies and frequently attack people—for example, in certain parts of India or Romania?[8] What if it happens in an impoverished neighborhood where dogs have been known to steal food from the plates of malnourished children? If you grew up in a place like this, the sight of a dog might scare you, and you might actually be relieved that this person kicked the dog out of your path. Even if you believe that it is inhumane to kick an animal for any reason, you now have some insight into why that person kicked the dog.

SO WHAT?

We may not like the way other people act or what they believe, but suspending judgment and considering the possible roots of the behavior is the first step to recognizing the diverse ways in which people around the globe have been culturally programmed. Armed with this new information, your reaction to a situation and how you handle it may shift.

This example about the dog usually elicits the strongest reactions from people. It also underscores how our perceptions and responses can change only when we expand our frames of reference.

Programmed to Perceive

We've already established that people perceive and reenact animal noises differently across cultures, and that those perceptions can be hard to shake. But let's move beyond moos and baas.

Take a look at Figure 1.2. What do you see?

The point of this exercise is to demonstrate that once we see something in a certain way, it is difficult to see it another way. If we get stuck after seeing these images just once, imagine how stuck we would

See the old woman? How about the young woman looking off to the side? They're both there. The old woman's mouth doubles as the young woman's choker necklace. The young woman's jawline is the old woman's nose. Even after being exposed to this drawing multiple times, people have difficulty seeing both faces.

Figure 1.2: Seeing and believing

get if we saw only one of the faces over and over again and no one ever noticed or mentioned the other face. After months and years of continual reinforcement, the chances of your discovering the other face on your own would be slim. Now, imagine how challenging it could be if you've heard, seen, believed, or done something a particular way your whole life and then were asked to perceive it another way.

Another thing about perceptions that trips us up when we interact with people from other cultures is the lack of a frame of reference for behaviors we've never seen before. Just as we might have missed seeing one face or the other in Figure 1.2, think about all of the cultural nuances that we might be missing just because our brains have not been primed to recognize them. This is one aspect of a phenomenon referred to in academic circles as "perceptual blindness."[9]

For many years a story has been circulating about the Europeans' initial approach of the New World, which illustrates this notion of perceptual blindness. According to one account, the Native Americans could not see Christopher Columbus's tall ships in the distance even though they were staring straight at them. One theory is that they couldn't see the ships because it was incomprehensible to them that boats of that size could exist. Another theory is that they observed the ships, but couldn't even begin to identify these hulking shapes.[10]

Although the validity of these accounts is a bit dubious, there are other documented examples of this particular kind of perceptual blindness, including one by the American inventor Thomas Edison.

Edison made a curious observation when he beta tested the phonograph, which was first developed to play back recordings of people speaking. When he pulled random people off the street, none of whom had heard of the phonograph before, and played them a recording of a simple sentence, most people couldn't make out what was being said. No matter how many times he played it, they still couldn't understand it. But if the person was told what was being said in the recording, they would be able to hear it clearly the next time they listened.

This account was chronicled by Edison biographer Randall Stross, who also included Edison's own speculation about what had occurred: "They do not expect or imagine that a machine can talk hence cannot understand it[s] words."

Stross also noted that that the same phenomenon was observed when people used a telephone for the first time.[11]

These observations illustrate how our brains can be a little slow on the uptake when we are so utterly unfamiliar with something. When we cross cultures, lack of contextual reference points can easily jostle our mental operating system. Although sometimes we take these moments in stride, more often than not they will trigger emotions such as surprise, wonder, confusion, and even anger.

Consider the simple act of slurping your soup, for example. When I was growing up, slurping at the dinner table was considered an unacceptable behavior that my mother was always quick to silence. So you can imagine my shock the first time I dined at a restaurant with a Japanese colleague who fervently sucked up her noodles. I was still somewhat appalled, even though I knew that slurping is an expected and appreciated sign that someone is enjoying his or her food. But imagine how appalled I would have been if I didn't know that slurping was considered good manners.

When perceptions have been reinforced throughout our lives, we stop paying close attention to them. In our daily lives we make unconscious split-second assumptions about what we are seeing and what things mean.

Try reading the phrases in Figure 1.3 and you'll see what I mean.

Our minds do this because they are hardwired to minimize effort, automating our perceptions so that we can devote mental energy to other things.[12] But if we just allow our perceptions and interpretations to run on autopilot without considering other frames of reference, we're likely to run into trouble on the cross-cultural playing field. And although training your mind to expand its frame of reference

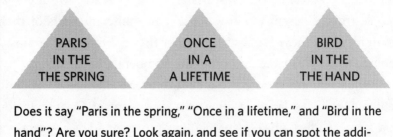

Does it say "Paris in the spring," "Once in a lifetime," and "Bird in the hand"? Are you sure? Look again, and see if you can spot the additional articles (redundant appearances of "the" and "a"). In this case we are interpreting language based on our assumptions, but consider how our brains fill in the gaps for us in countless other situations.

Figure 1.3: Reading and believing

is doable, it's no small feat, considering what we've learned in recent years about how culture *literally* shapes our brains.

Our Brains on Culture

People from different cultures tend to look different from each other. I'm talking about physical appearance: things like skin, hair, facial features, and so on. This is not news. What is newsworthy is that our brains look different too.

Emerging evidence from a new field of research known as *cultural neuroscience* is just beginning to shed light on how culture physically molds our brains. Our respective cultures forge neural pathways in distinctive patterns, organizing our brain functions in ways not previously thought possible.

Neuroscientists have long believed that each cognitive function—such as seeing, listening, analytical thinking, and emotional response—occurs in the same distinct areas of all brains. But through the use of fMRI (functional magnetic resonance imaging) scans and other brain-imaging technology, researchers have been able to show that people from different cultures actually use different parts of their brain for all of these functions, whether they are listening to music, looking at people's faces, or crunching numbers.[13]

"When you are exposed to a culture over a lifetime, your brain reorganizes," says Jamshed Bharucha, president of Cooper Union and former Tufts University psychology professor. "The connections between the neurons change, then the brain develops these cultural lenses through which you perceive the world."[14]

Recent research has revealed that culture can even override genetics, including a predisposition to depression. Former Northwestern University psychologist Joan Chiao discovered that a disproportionate number of people from East Asian cultures have a genetic trait that makes them more susceptible to depression than people from the United States, yet Americans have a much higher incidence of depression. This puzzling discovery lead Chiao to conclude that the collectivist nature of East Asian cultures could affect the way that depression genes express themselves. In other words, being a more group-oriented culture may help stop depression from manifesting in individuals. Chiao also speculates that collectivist instincts may have actually coevolved with genetic traits, as a means of offsetting the tendency toward depression.[15]

While studies like these are starting to reveal how deeply culture affects our minds, that doesn't mean that we are all forever destined to think or act in certain ways. Our cultural programming creates habits, and just like the many personal habits we accumulate over the course of our lives that we may try to alter—from cracking knuckles to smoking cigarettes—culturally induced habits are deeply forged and hard to shake. In some ways, cultural habits may be even tougher to break, because everyone else in our community is doing them too. And because we aren't even aware of them. But there are pathways to changing almost any kind of habit once we become aware of it.[16]

As an example, consider the case of Korean Air, whose poor safety record and numerous crashes in the 1990s seems likely to have stemmed from cultural programming related to hierarchy. Brought to the public's attention by Malcolm Gladwell's book *Outliers*, there was a widespread belief that the Korean copilots were afraid to point out mistakes or disagree with the captain because their deeply embedded cultural programming dictated that they defer to the judgment of their superiors. Gladwell also notes that the sophisticated planes they were flying were intended to be piloted by a flight crew working as equals, not a single leader.[17]

According to one of the pioneers of cultural neuroscience, the late Tufts psychology professor Nalini Ambady, Korean Air pilots have since succeeded in modifying some of those cultural reflexes that may have compromised their performance and jeopardized lives. Today, Korean Air's record is in fact greatly improved. "What cultural neuroscience shows," said Ambady, "is that the brain is not fixed—it's malleable."[18]

While the benefits can be vast, changing your cultural habits is admittedly not simple. There is, however, a three-step method that you can apply in many situations to enhance your ability to curb your cultural reflexes. It's the same method I share with all of my clients:

1. Recognize your own cultural programming.

2. Open your mind to other ways of perceiving or approaching a situation.

3. Adjust your response to optimize results.

The more you sift through your cultural baggage and recognize your own cultural programming (step #1), the easier it will become to put the next two steps into action. Getting to the bottom of your bag won't happen overnight. I've been at it for several decades, and I still regularly discover new aspects of my cultural programming.

But now that your own process of self-discovery is under way, you're ready to take the next step and open your mind to other ways of thinking (step #2), following in the footsteps of intrepid anthropologists and a Dutch guy from IBM.

Breaking It Down: The Dimensions of Culture

Although revelations from the field of cultural neuroscience are undoubtedly exciting and enlightening, we don't need brain scans to hack our cultural "coding," thanks to decades of work by experts who have studied the effects of culture and devised maps to help guide us through this convoluted terrain.

The first explorers were cultural anthropologists like Margaret Mead and Franz Boas, whose studies helped demystify the lives of little-known indigenous peoples around the globe—and whose observations and methodical analyses helped form the basis of the modern-day investigations. Next came the interculturalists, whose studies focused in on the way that cultures relate to one another—a field usually attributed to the work of pioneering anthropologist Edward Hall in the 1950s and '60s. Hall's work spawned a generation of intercultural experts and analysts who dedicated themselves to figuring out how a greater understanding of cultural differences could be used to achieve a variety of goals, from diplomacy to sales to organizational effectiveness.

The earliest and most widely known studies of the intersection between business and culture were conducted at IBM by a Dutch industrial psychologist named Geert Hofstede. Starting in 1965, Hofstede worked in-house with international colleagues to assess the attitudes of IBM's workers around the globe, hoping the results would reveal how to improve company productivity. His background was perfect for the job; he was not only a social scientist but also a mechanical engineer (so he understood technical lingo), and he had spent time working at different kinds of factories, from hosiery to textiles. He could also converse in five languages—Dutch, English, French, German, and Italian—all of which he began learning in Dutch grade school in the 1940s.

At IBM, Hofstede and his colleagues conducted "attitude" surveys with employees from forty different countries, all of whom were asked the same questions. As the results of the surveys began to amass and analysis got under way, he noticed that attitudes and associated behaviors seemed to play out along cultural lines. Intrigued by his findings, Hofstede took a sabbatical from IBM to do more research at a university in Lausanne, Switzerland, where he eventually took a teaching position and continued to analyze the data. In 1980 he published his findings in a book, *Culture's Consequences*. In 1991 he came out with a lay version (although still fairly academic): *Cultures and Organizations: Software of the Mind*. It became an international best seller.

In a nutshell, Hofstede was among the first to offer proof that national and regional groupings (cultures) affect the behavior of people within organizations. Although his findings have been questioned for reasons such as the fact that his research was mostly limited to white males, it brought wider attention and credence to the impacts of culture on organizations. It provided a starting point for conversations about an understudied subject with vast implications for business, political diplomacy, and, now, for life in our global communities.

Hofstede also became known for the way that he broke down behaviors into five categories or *dimensions*, as they are often referred to. Unlike the dimensions described by Hall and other scholars who came before him, Hofstede's take was more directly applicable to the needs of businesses and organizations. In Hofstede's initial study, these dimensions included matters like whether people place an emphasis on hierarchy or equality, whether they embrace uncertainty or avoid it, whether they are generally more concerned with individual needs or with group harmony, and whether they value traditional male attributes such as assertiveness and competitiveness or stereotypical female traits such as being nurturing and cultivating relationships.[19]

Within each dimension, people fell along a spectrum, from those who demonstrated extreme attitudes (either very individualistic or very group oriented, for example) to those who acted in ways that were more middle of the road. Of course, Hofstede recognized that there were exceptional people who fell outside his theoretical spectrums. The inexact nature of his theories sparked controversy, but his findings also prompted much-needed inquiry.

Over the years many scholars have continued to refine, expand upon, and adapt the notion of dimensions to suit the needs of different communities. No version is right or wrong; culture is a vast and amorphous subject area that warrants being poked from all sides.

The next six chapters of this book present my own riff on the dimensions of culture that highlight tendencies I believe will provide the most benefits to people today—tendencies that have the greatest influence on how we communicate and interact with people from other cultures at work and in everyday life. As you delve into each cross-cultural topic, you'll begin to acquire a new awareness of the wide range of perceptions, beliefs, and values that influence people's behaviors. You'll also come away with a set of applicable skills for navigating cross-cultural interactions in different circumstances.

Each of the topics I cover is worthy of its own book, and there are plenty of other important topics that warrant deep investigation, like cultural views of gender. But the point of this book is to provide an introduction to the many ways that culture impacts you and everyone with whom you interact, helping establish a solid foundation on which to launch your deeper dives into specific topics and cultures.

The Case for Generalizations

In many circumstances, making generalizations is a bad idea. It can lead to the development of prejudices, which in turn can lead to all sorts of negative fallout. When it comes to understanding cultural differences, however, a little of the right kind of generalizing can go a long way toward better understanding.

There is no denying that certain groups of people tend to share similar sets of ideologies and associated behaviors. That's not to say that every person within a culture acts the same way or believes the same things. For example, not all Germans have a relatively direct style of communication, nor are all Japanese people indirect communicators. But there is a great tendency for people from those cultures to act one way or another. As a native New Yorker, my wife grew up with people who were very direct communicators. "You could use a haircut" or "How do you get away with charging that much for a cup of coffee?" are the kind of statements regularly issued by some of her old friends. They act in a way that seems in accordance with the tendency of people from New York to be direct. Does this mean that they are always direct? Of course not. Are there New Yorkers we know who tend to be more or less direct? Certainly.

People exhibit shared cultural traits to varying degrees and in different ways depending on the circumstance and individual personality traits, among other factors. Cultural generalizations merely offer a starting point for figuring people out. Most Korean people eat with chopsticks. Many Swiss people are punctual. Brazilians often show up late to social functions. Taken out of context or laden with judgment, these statements can be construed as offensive, but as a comparative tool for anticipating how someone is most likely to behave—and correctly interpreting the behavior—generalizations are indispensable.

Although they do not ring true in every case, calling attention to the tendencies of certain groups of people reminds us to consider other ways of thinking. The stories and statements I've included in this book are meant to be deconstructed, challenged, and applied in thoughtful ways. Any generalizations are intended to help you open your mind, not close it.

TWO

Me or We?

Recognize the differences between group and individual orientation, and why it matters

On a balmy July afternoon in 2002, more than forty thousand U.S. baseball fans flocked to Milwaukee's Miller Park to attend a highly anticipated Major League All-Star game. Legends such as Hank Aaron and Willie Mays were being honored, while superstars like Cal Ripken Jr. and Barry Bonds competed on the field. After eleven innings, the game finished "amid a sea of boos" when a 7–7 tie was called. Both teams had simply run out of pitchers.[1]

Players, fans, and the press were all outraged by the tie score. According to one ESPN reporter, "the outcry was such that you would have thought commissioner Bud Selig had walked to the mound and dropped puppies one by one into a vat of boiling water."[2] It's often recalled as one of the most disappointing games in U.S. baseball history.

Ties had already been outlawed in regular season games, but as a result of what happened in Milwaukee, the rules were changed so that ties would no longer be permissible in All-Star games either.[3] In the United States, a tie game in any sport is generally considered not only frustrating but also boring. Former professional football coach Eddie Erdelatz summed it up neatly when he issued his memorable remark: "A tie is like kissing your sister." It's just no fun.

In Japan, however, where baseball also has long been a national obsession, professional games can and do end in ties.[4] These tie games rarely elicit outrage or audible boos. That's not to say that fans don't want their team to win, but a tie may be considered an equally acceptable outcome: everybody wins, no one bears the shame of loss, and everyone gets to bed at a reasonable time.

The stark contrast between American and Japanese reactions to tie games is rooted in some fundamental cultural differences related to the way we think about ourselves and the people who surround us.

Essentially, Japanese people tend to be more focused on the well-being, success, and harmony of the group (what I refer to as a "We" ideology), while people from the United States tend to be more focused on individual well-being and success (a "Me" ideology).

Tie games aren't the only way that different Me/We tendencies play out in baseball. Another big difference relates to how people cheer. In Japan, only fans sitting in a special cheering section called an *endan* hoot and holler in response to what's happening on the field. Without the endan, the stadium can be as quiet as a cemetery, as star baseball player Ichiro Suzuki attests after having spent time playing on both Japanese and American teams: "I think Japanese fans, like the Japanese players, suppress their emotions too. They are very *otonash* (quiet). You have the cheerleaders blowing trumpets and all. But when they're not doing anything, the stadium is really quiet. American fans, by contrast, do their own thing—people stand up and dance. The fans get up and express themselves, they show their own individuality, just like the players."[5]

Fans at a Japanese baseball game are also likely to stick around and help clean up after a game. Yep, you read that right. They clean up that sticky, soupy, garbage-strewn mess that most of us try to ignore and avoid as we exit the stadium. Fans rarely, if ever, clean up the stands at a professional-level U.S. game. The conscientious behavior of Japanese fans isn't unique to baseball; Japanese spectators shocked fans from around the world when they stuck around to clean up the mess after a rainy World Cup soccer game, in which Japan lost to Ivory Coast.[6] It's something Japanese fans often do after all national soccer games.

But enough about sports. We and Me ideologies can affect many facets of our lives, from the way we network, to the way we sell products (and sell ourselves), to the way we are motivated to succeed. For example, did you attend a school where students were lauded as "top of the class," valedictorian, or its equivalent? According to a recent *Forbes* article, more than 80 percent of U.S. companies motivate people through awards like "employee of the month" or "top salesperson."[7] In Me societies this kind of public recognition of individual activities and one-time achievements is often a driving force throughout people's lives.[8] Whether the recognition comes in the form of a blue ribbon or a pile of cash, the glory of being named "the best" is dangled before some of us like a golden carrot, from our first piano recital to our last chili cook-off.

Cultures that are more toward the We end of the spectrum are usually more likely to discourage standing out from the crowd.[9] People may only rarely be publicly singled out at school or at work. Greater satisfaction may be derived from supporting the achievements of a team, class, or group—or the entire country.

If you are from a Me culture, imagine how it would feel to take individual recognition out of the mix at the workplace. Would that throw you into a tailspin? Most Westerners (myself included) are programmed to expect that if they come up with an idea, they will get credit for it in some way. If someone else—like a manager—took credit for my idea, I would feel disrespected and cheated out of a potential bonus or promotion.

Now consider this: in We-leaning cultures, letting your boss or whole team take credit for your work is fairly common and considered totally acceptable. The idea is, it doesn't matter whose idea it was as long the whole group benefits and harmony is maintained. In We cultures, individual promotions and bonuses are more likely to be doled out based on team longevity than on individual achievements.

Not surprisingly, how we view and talk about our achievements is influenced by our Me/We orientation. Nowhere is this more apparent then in the interview process. If you were to interview in a Me culture like the United States, the first thing the interviewer might say to you is, "So tell me about yourself." You would probably spend most of your time talking with pride about your experience and accomplishments and all the things that you as an individual can bring to the table. Eventually, after your monologue ended, the interviewer would offer some remarks about your achievements and how they might mesh with the job requirements. You would probably use body language and tone to reflect strong self-confidence and enthusiasm; you might strive to project a casual and comfortable air, and you would try to make a point of asking questions.

If you were to interview for a job in a We culture, the conversation might follow a different track. When you talk about your experiences, instead of simply itemizing all of your individual achievements, you would probably be expected to place more emphasis on how you've worked as a team member to achieve success in the past. It might be prudent to highlight examples that illustrate your willingness to sacrifice personal needs for a group or company's benefit. You might use body language and silence to show that you are listening and thinking deeply about questions before answering them. Projecting a certain air of humility would likely be well received.

Here's the rub: if you didn't know that expectations like these can vary across cultures, you wouldn't be able to figure out what behaviors are expected, and your likelihood of getting the job would be diminished for all the wrong reasons. This is a prime example of *unconscious incompetence*. Similarly, if you are the person conducting the interview, you might write off an excellent candidate simply based on a misinterpretation of how the candidate presented him- or herself. This is what academics call an *unconscious bias*. It refers to assumptions and interpretations you make about another person's behaviors—assumptions that you are not even aware of. For example, you might perceive a job candidate from a Me culture as too boastful, or someone from a We culture as lacking in confidence, based on your perception of what you observe. We all associate certain behaviors and language with the traits of confidence, passion, energy, and intelligence. When we don't see or hear those associated cues, we are more apt to write someone off as not possessing those qualities.

Through my work with both large and small companies around the globe, I've witnessed unconscious biases affect the hiring process over and over again. Today, companies everywhere are looking to tap the burgeoning economies in places like China, India, and Russia, and they need to hire talented people from those countries and others to help them do it. By going with their gut instincts (leading with the unconscious), interviewers are more likely to overlook good candidates. For the company doing the hiring, it can be a major missed opportunity. For the candidate, it's a frustrating rejection. Everybody loses. The good news is that if you simply prime yourself to consider how interview behaviors can be interpreted differently across cultures and do a little pre-interview investigation, you open the door to all sorts of opportunities, no matter which side of the interview table you are sitting on.

Behaviors and perceptions that are influenced by Me-We ideologies are drummed into our minds from an early age. When my daughter was ready to attend preschool, my wife and I purposefully chose a school with a low student-to-teacher ratio (about six to one), based on our desire for her to get as much individualized attention as possible. Like many others in the United States, we are conditioned to place a premium on small class sizes. As our daughter's education continues, we gather with other parents and ponder whether the large

size of public school classes is limiting our children's academic success. Small class size is one of the reasons people shell out big bucks
for private school.

Now consider that in Japan, the ideal preschooler-to-teacher ratio
is anywhere from *twenty-three to thirty* to one. Although this ratio also
occurs in Western public schools, nobody considers it ideal; neither
the parents nor the teachers who struggle to keep all those wriggly
bodies and distracted minds under control. But that's exactly the point.

The thinking behind the high ratio is that it helps children learn
how to interact harmoniously with others, *without* adult interven-
tion. Although academics are extremely important, this social skill is
imperative to any kind of success in the We-focused Japanese society.

In a *New York Times* editorial, columnist Nicholas Kristof wrote
this account of living in Japan with his children. It illustrates some of
the ways that kids are habituated to We ideology:

> My wife and I saw the collective ethos drummed into children when we
> sent our kids to Japanese schools. When the teacher was sick, there
> was no substitute teacher. The children were in charge. When our son
> Gregory came home from a school athletic meet, we were impressed
> that he had won first place in all his events, until we realized that every
> child had won first place. For Gregory's birthday, we invited his
> classmates over and taught them to play musical chairs. Disaster! The
> children, especially the girls, were traumatized by having to push aside
> others to gain a seat for themselves. What unfolded may have been
> the most polite, most apologetic, and least competitive game of
> musical chairs in the history of the world.[10]

Driving the Japanese kids' behavior in this game of musical chairs
was a desire to maintain harmony and, more specifically, to make sure
no one felt bad about being left out. They wanted everyone to be able
to *save face*. You've probably heard the expression "save face" before
and have a rough idea of what it means, but you may be surprised to

learn how critical it is in certain cultures and the many different ways it can play out.

All About Face

The concept of face relates to recognizing the dignity, honor, and reputation of an individual or group. The notion of *saving* face refers to the idea of preserving those elements. Essentially it's about avoiding public embarrassment or shame for either ourselves, another person, or an entire group. There's also the concept of *gaining* face, which refers to enhancing a person's (or group's) reputation.

Face plays a particularly important role in many We-oriented cultures, shaping behaviors and perceptions in every aspect of people's lives. Face is also relevant in Me cultures, but it usually doesn't carry as much significance or have as much bearing on the way people conduct themselves.

For example, in We cultures, disagreeing with someone's ideas might imply that you dislike them personally, so someone might act as if they agree with you even if they don't, just to avoid damaging the relationship. The fear of losing face can deter people from expressing opinions in group settings where they might unwittingly offend someone. The profound desire to preserve face in some cultures can drive people to avoid confrontations at all costs.

This kind of behavior certainly occurs in Me cultures too, but much less frequently, and disagreeing with someone is far less likely to be construed as a personal affront or to jeopardize a relationship. In Me cultures, expressing personal opinions in a group setting is more likely to be permissible and is often encouraged. People are more likely to initiate a confrontation with the hope that the issue can be resolved and everyone can move on quickly.

So what happens when people from a face-focused culture have to confront people from a culture in which face doesn't play a critical role (or vice versa)?

Consider what happened April 2001, when a U.S. Navy aircraft and a Chinese fighter literally collided over Chinese airspace, causing the death of a Chinese pilot. The U.S. aircraft had to make an emergency landing, and the crew was detained and interrogated by the Chinese authorities for the next eleven days. Why did it take so long for the crew to be released? The Chinese were looking for an apology, but the U.S. official explained, "We did not do anything wrong, and therefore it was not possible to apologize."[11]

After much tense deliberation, the U.S. ambassador delivered a letter to the Chinese foreign minister, and the crew was promptly released. The Chinese claimed it was a letter of apology; a U.S. senior administration official was quoted as saying "What the Chinese will choose to characterize as an apology, we would probably choose to characterize as an expression of regret or sorrow." The letter was worded in a way that allowed both countries to save face.

This kind of "face diplomacy" can be just as important in business transactions as it is in international affairs. One of my clients who sells homes in master planned communities described an unpleasant encounter he had with a real estate agent from a face-focused culture who was trying to get a better deal for his buyers.

The agent arrived at the home with the buyers that he was representing and did a walk-through of the house they were about to purchase. As they toured the home, the agent continually made requests for things like extended counter tops, an upgraded garage, or a bigger stove, all of which were politely rebuffed by the salesman because those options were simply not available for this home model. After the fifth failed request, the agent became extremely agitated; he slammed his hand down on the salesperson's clipboard and demanded that there be some discount.

Although the agent's reaction was clearly extreme, chances are that he acted out for fear of losing face in front of his customers. He was failing to get a better deal. The salesperson handled it deftly: he left the room, giving the agent and buyers time to continue exploring the house. When they were ready to leave, the agent said to the salesperson: "No hard feelings. Just doing business. Let's go to lunch next week." It was as if the agent's theatrics were all just part of a show he was putting on for the buyers.

Going to lunch was the last thing the salesperson wanted to do (and he didn't), but it was probably the best thing he could have done. Lunch could have been an opportunity to strengthen the relationship. The agent and salesperson could discuss how they could approach a similar situation next time so that nobody would lose face in front of a customer. If they do it right, they might even *gain* face. I've seen strategically orchestrated scenarios unfold in which an agent has to ask for something multiple times before the request is finally granted. This bit of theater allows the agent to gain face in front of his or her customers and can strengthen relationships all around.

I share this anecdote to illustrate how the desire to save face can influence people's behaviors in ways that might be surprising to someone from a more Me-oriented culture. When face is a driving force, people may go to seemingly great lengths to preserve and enhance it. When a failure or mistake causes someone to lose face, their sense of shame might seem disproportionate to someone from a Me culture yet is in perfect synch with public perceptions and expectations from certain We-leaning cultures.

In extreme cases, the shame associated with a loss of face may feel unbearable. Students in We-leaning cultures like India, China, and South Korea are among the most likely to take their own lives after doing poorly on university entrance exams, rather than incur a loss of face for themselves or their families.[12] At universities like Cornell University and MIT, recent studies have shown that a disproportionate number of Asian and Asian Americans take their lives each year; many of them probably folded under the pressures connected to fear of losing face.[13]

In some cultures, suicide can be considered an acceptable exit from a disgraceful situation. It is a means of saving face for someone's family, company, community, or even country.[14] In Japan, the practice used to be so widely accepted that there was even a suicide manual on their best seller list back in the 1990s.[15]

I don't mean to suggest that this is a common practice, or that you might inadvertently do something that could cause someone to take their own life. This occurs only in extreme situations. It's also important to note that there are no more suicides per capita in We-leaning countries than Me-leaning countries. I share these examples with you simply to illustrate how important saving face is in certain cultures.

Passed down from generation to generation and reinforced throughout our lives, the notion of face can affect everything from how people play musical chairs and baseball to how they conduct themselves at work and in their communities. Face can affect people in ways they are barely aware of, influencing how they make decisions, take risks, build business and social networks, and countless other things—including how people perceive themselves.

Risk, Reputation, and Relationships

While the notion of having a good reputation is important across many cultures, the way people go about preserving and enhancing their reputation can be totally different. Take failure, for example. In a Me culture, failure can compromise someone's reputation in the short term, but it can often be repaired through future successes. A good example of this attitude toward failure can be seen in Silicon Valley, a subset of U.S. culture wherein failure is a totally acceptable part of the process. The concept of "failing forward" has spread to U.S. schools, where students are encouraged to take greater risks and embrace failure as part of the learning process.

In We-leaning cultures, on the other hand, risk taking tends to be encouraged only when it is highly calculated, because the stigma of failure can be difficult to shake. Fear of failure and the resulting loss of face can make people in We cultures less likely to embrace all kinds of changes—whether in their personal lives or in business. Sticking to the status quo minimizes these risks and ensures that reputations will be preserved intact.

When it comes to building a good reputation, differences can also play out along Me-We lines. While a good reputation in Me cultures often hinges solely on individual achievement, in We cultures reputations are more often based on someone's contributions to the well-being of an organization or community.

While people from both sides of the spectrum might be inclined to offer help to a neighbor with their garden or assist a colleague with a report, people from We cultures may perceive it as an expected social duty, whereas Me-leaning people may see it as an exceptional personal sacrifice. In Me cultures, the same level of "self-sacrifice" is not necessary to build relationships and could even be construed as overbearing or intrusive behavior.

I found myself on the receiving end of this kind of gesture a few years ago when I traveled to Saudi Arabia to deliver a weeklong leadership workshop for employees of a large multinational company. During my day off, a participant from the region offered to pick me up and show me around the city. This was his day off to spend with his family, so I politely refused. But he insisted. After going back and forth a few times, I eventually acquiesced, and that morning we explored the local souks together. Around midday I suggested that I return to my hotel so he could spend the rest of the day with his family. He declined again, and generously continued on as my tour guide into the evening hours. As if that wasn't enough, on the last day of my stay in Saudi Arabia he brought me a sampling of some traditional cuisine, apologizing that the restaurant that served it had been closed during the day he showed me around.

Besides being tremendously grateful for all that this man did for me during my stay, I was also awestruck. From my perspective it was not expected or even remotely necessary. It was even somewhat overwhelming, coming from a stranger. But it was his way of showing appreciation for the work that I was doing. Having done business in this part of the world over the past decade, I knew that for me to have firmly refused would have been disappointing to him—perhaps even causing him to lose face.

In many Me-leaning cultures, this kind of experience would fall into the category of a noteworthy act of kindness. I suspect that the man who showed me around Riyadh didn't think what he did was particularly remarkable. Over the course of my career I've experienced similar feats of hospitality, most of which have occurred in We-leaning cultures. As a result, I've become much more at ease with and accepting of this kind of generosity. I also try to return the generosity and meet this social expectation when people from those cultures visit me in the United States—doing my best to override my Me instincts, which would normally lead me to prioritize my individual needs and tasks over tending to social relations.

Although it may not have been necessary for me to reciprocate, if I ever had an opportunity to offer the same hospitality to the man in Riyadh it could potentially take our relationship to the next level, cementing a spot in each other's social networks and conferring a variety of benefits in each of our respective cultural contexts.

Expanding and Maintaining Our Networks

Our web of personal connections creates the foundation for our lives as social creatures, no matter what culture we come from. But *how* and *why* we choose to build and expand our networks is often in step with Me and We orientations. Think about why you would want to add someone to your network. In Me cultures, connections are often made to accomplish a specific task, like finding a babysitter or candidates for a job. Sometimes it's because the person has a particular expertise that is relevant to our own work, personal interests, or communities. These connections are often established—and set aside—fairly quickly, requiring little maintenance.

In We cultures, you might be more likely to add someone to your network because of their group affiliations than for their individual expertise or achievements. The networking goal is more likely to be about developing deep and long-term strategic relationships than for completing short-term tasks. In these cultures, where group dynamics are paramount, the process of building networks tends to be much more elaborate, well defined, and long term. Developing these networks—and the influence that they afford—is often more critical to success in We cultures than in Me cultures.

In China, for example, the art of networking in business revolves around a system of building social capital known as *guanxi* ("gwanshee"). Loosely translated as "relationships," your guanxi is the measure of how strong your individual relationships are and how many relations you have. The process of gaining and growing guanxi requires perseverance and strategic foresight. Guanxi is largely accrued through a process in which two people—or two companies—offer and request services from each other on an ongoing basis. Inherent in the guanxi building process is the expectation that these requests for services or favors will not be refused—and that both parties have an obligation to maintain the relationship. If you don't reciprocate, it may cause the other person to lose face and, in turn, you lose an opportunity to build guanxi.

I received my first lesson in guanxi building years ago while traveling in China with a group of American teachers as part of a cultural exchange. At an inaugural banquet staged by local officials, I spent several hours chatting and drinking bai-jo (a potent liquor) with a Chinese dignitary. The next morning the young nephew of my drinking partner showed up in my hotel lobby. The boy had been instructed to accompany me for the next three weeks so that he could learn English.

Unbeknownst to me, guanxi building was underway: hosting the banquet was the local official's first offering to me; teaching the nephew English would be the return favor. But I wasn't able to let the nephew tag along for more than a day, feeling put upon by the request and unknowingly terminating the bid for guanxi. Had I been able to oblige, the reciprocity probably would have continued, with each of us benefiting from the other's sphere of influence.

The process of building guanxi can go on for many years: like cultivating a garden, it's something that must be consistently maintained in order for it to continue to grow and bear fruit throughout your life. If your guanxi garden lies dormant for a while, you may have to start again from scratch.

Systems like guanxi are not unique to China. In many parts of the Arab world, for example, there is the concept of *wasta*—a term for the ability to use one's connections and influence to get things done. Similar systems exist in countries throughout Latin America, like Colombia and Mexico, where they call this kind of social capital *palanca*. In Brazil it's called *jeito*.

Differences in the way people build connections play out in other ways too, like on social media platforms (how quickly do you add someone to your LinkedIn network or friend them on Facebook?) and in the hiring process (how many meetings are required before hiring someone?).

How we organize and maintain our family networks can also divide along Me-We lines. A few years ago the director of marketing of a U.S. home building company reached out to me because his team was having trouble selling homes designed for multigenerational families. The houses had semi-detached in-law units, complete with a private bedroom and bathroom and kitchen/eating space. Each unit had a door connecting it to the main house and another one that exited to the side of the house, allowing privacy and independence. The floor plan was popular with people native to the United States, but not with more recent immigrants from India and Vietnam.

It occurred to me that the houses weren't selling because of the We orientation of the prospective buyers. Perhaps all of the privacy and separation features that Me-leaning people loved were actually a turn-off to people from these other cultures. What if they actually wanted a floor plan designed to foster a more communal living experience, featuring things like two master suites inside the main house and an extra-large kitchen/dining area? A few months later the home-building company decided to start offering homes with this We-inspired configuration, and as hoped, more people began buying them.

We can't possibly know all the ins and outs of how others expect to build and maintain business, personal, and familial relationships, but we can get familiar with the range of possibilities—and more importantly, recognize our own habits, preferences, and perceptions.

Are You a Me or a We?

Getting a sense of where you fall on the Me-We spectrum in relation to people from other cultures can be challenging. It's easier to judge ourselves relative to the people with whom we interact regularly, but even that can be difficult to assess. The best way to begin sizing up your Me-ness or We-ness is by thinking about how you act in certain scenarios. Answering the five questions that follow is a simple way to kick off your self-investigation process. Try to answer them based on your first impulse, without spending time thinking about how your response might change in certain contexts or depending on your relationship with others involved. While these details do matter, the idea is just to get a general sense of your tendencies as a starting point.

ME-WE SELF TEST

1. You've done most of the work on a group project at work or school, yet everybody on the team gets credit for a job well done. Your thoughts are ...

a. What the heck? I do all the work and then everybody else gets the credit? I'm letting my manager/teacher know.

b. No big deal. At least the project turned out well.

c. I'm glad the team was recognized for a job well done.

2. You are walking down the street and someone asks you for directions to a place that's about a quarter mile away (and you know where it is). You ...

a. Tell them you don't know.

b. Verbally describe how to get there.

c. Personally escort them to the place.

3. You are recognized by your company as one of the monthly "superstars," and your picture and accomplishments are featured in a newsletter. You feel ...

a. Proud and happy to be recognized.

b. It's nice to be recognized, but seems like an unnecessary amount of public acknowledgment.

c. Very embarrassed and uncomfortable receiving all of the attention.

4. You disagree with a strategy proposed by a colleague (someone of equal rank) during an internal staff meeting. You ...

a. Tell them why you disagree with them right then and there.

b. Remain silent during the meeting, then discuss your reason for disagreeing privately at a later time.

c. Say that you think it's a fine idea, and leave it at that.

5. You've been an employee at a company for several months. You come up with a simple idea that could help your company make more money. You ...

a. Begin to implement it.

b. Share the idea with your boss.

c. Share the idea with as many colleagues as possible to gather their thoughts and build consensus before even bringing it to your boss.

To find out where you fall on the Me-We spectrum, review your answers and give yourself zero points for every "a" answer, one point for every "b" answer, and two points for every "c." Then see where your total falls in this scale:

0   1   2   3   4   5   6   7   8   9   10

Me   We

As noted earlier, this is just an exercise to get you thinking about how your Me-We programming influences your behaviors and expectations. For most people, tendencies will tilt toward different ends of the spectrum depending on the situation, but people from certain cultures do consistently lean more toward Me or We in most scenarios.

Before we explore where specific cultures tend to fall on the Me-We spectrum, it's useful to spend a little more time considering how your own programming can influence the way that you interpret—or misinterpret—the actions of people from other cultures. For example, people from Me-oriented cultures often assume the people from We cultures are too passive and lack confidence, ambition, and passion. Why do they think this? Here are some commonly observed behaviors that can lead to this assumption:

- Not speaking up enough in group settings like meetings
- Frequently seeking feedback from others
- Being unable to make decisions quickly
- Deferring to group choices rather than staying committed to their own ideas

Conversely, many people from We cultures may jump to the conclusion that people from Me cultures are selfish, rash, disrespectful, and arrogant. Here are some behaviors that can make them think this:

- Making decisions without first getting group feedback
- Speaking and acting relatively quickly
- Frequently interrupting in group settings and not pausing to listen to others
- Being motivated more by individual recognition/reward than by group progress
- Not seeming to care too much about what others think
- Openly teasing or making fun of each other—even the boss

If and when people make these assumptions about others, it's often because they are culturally programmed to perceive certain behaviors in particular ways—especially on first impression. Think about your own kneejerk reactions: If someone doesn't speak up during a meeting, is your first instinct to assume that person has nothing to contribute—or that they are being humble and polite by not interrupting everyone else? Do you perceive their behavior as positive or negative? In a flash, your brain performs a series of complex calisthenics based on past experience in order to make sense of what you are observing, and labels it so it can be neatly filed into your neural circuitry. The more we see the same behavior, the more our perceptions of that person are reinforced.

But these impressions are often inaccurate because they are formed based on incomplete information. The missing piece of info? Knowing whether someone is Me- or We-leaning and how that orientation affects his or her behaviors in various circumstances. The preceding list of typical Me-We meeting behaviors offers some clues to help you identify someone's orientation—and there are plenty of other clues that become apparent once you open your mind to them—but you'll never truly "get it" or connect with someone if you don't acknowledge the differing sets of beliefs and values that drive those behaviors. Scholars usually break down the differences in underlying beliefs and values in this way:

TYPICAL ME VALUES AND BELIEFS

- Individual achievement is valued over group accomplishments.

- Standing out from the group and being acknowledged is encouraged.

- Personal freedom and individual rights are paramount.

- Being a member of a specific group does *not* define who you are.

- Personal well-being is more important than the group's well-being.

- Completing individual tasks is given more emphasis than tending or building relationships.

TYPICAL WE VALUES AND BELIEFS

- The well-being of the group (company, family, country, and so on) is more important than personal well-being.

- The success of the group takes precedence over the individual's.

- Standing out from the group is looked down upon and discouraged.

- Group harmony, interdependence, and saving face are paramount.

- Being a member of a group is essential to one's identity, success, and, sometimes, survival.

- Tending or building relationships is given more emphasis than completing individual tasks.

Looking at these lists, it's easy to see why people from Me cultures usually recount experiences using "I" and "my" (even if it's a group experience), while people from We cultures tend to talk about their experiences using "we" and "our," and refer to friends and strangers alike in a familial way (as brother or sister, aunt or uncle), regardless of whether or not people are actually related. But there is no list of behaviors that unfailingly indicate that someone is from a Me or We culture. There are clues related to specific situations, like the ones related to meetings or building networks that I mention throughout the chapter— ultimately, it's just something that you have to feel your way through. But by simply becoming more aware of these different ideologies (and which ones drive your own behaviors), it becomes easier to spot the Me-We signs.

In the two sets of ideologies just listed, values and beliefs are lumped together in a very generalized way. Although many of these values, beliefs, and behaviors often go hand in hand, many cultures—and individuals within cultures—subscribe to a mix of typically Me or We ideologies to varying degrees. For example, people from the United States tend to focus more on tasks than on relationships at work, but they may prioritize nurturing relationships with friends and family over getting stuff done around the house. And although you may have been born and raised in a culture that tends toward individual or group-oriented ideologies, your personal preferences may differ.

Regardless of all the variables, there's no denying that certain national cultures tend to lean one way or another. Many scholarly and corporate studies have attempted to rank the Me-ness or We-ness of different cultures. Although the rating systems and rankings vary slightly from study to study, there are notable consistencies. For example, countries like England, Holland, the United States, and Australia are usually found at the far end of the Me side of the spectrum, while countries like Ecuador, Indonesia, and Ghana gather toward the We end. Countries like Turkey, Brazil, and India play leapfrog with each other in the middle (see Figure 1.4).

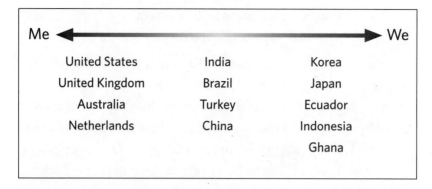

Figure 1.4: Country styles on the Me-We continuum

I'm often asked: Why have some countries evolved as more individualist and others as more collectivist? There is no single answer. The reasons vary from culture to culture and are often just theories. But it's still an interesting question that's worth exploring.

The United States consistently ranks as the number-one most Me-focused country. Why so individualistic? In the United States, this tendency probably has to do with the earliest European settlers who left their communities and set out on a journey into the unknown rather than compromise their personal beliefs. Their goal was to establish a new community where nobody would stop them from pursuing their individual callings. Today, their legacy is carried forward by the steady flow of immigrants and refugees who risk their lives in hope of reaching the United States, a place where they believe they have a better shot at forging their own path in life, in pursuit of some personal definition of success.

At the other end of the spectrum, there are a few theories about the origins of the We tendencies exhibited in certain cultures:

- Countries in which a significant number of people subscribe
  to Confucian philosophies (such as Korea, China, and Taiwan)
  are usually more We leaning,[16] probably because Confucianism
  places particular emphasis on the importance of social harmony.

This sentiment is epitomized in the Confucian proverb: "Do not do to others what you would not want others to do to you."

• Islamic-based cultures may be We leaning as a result of their religious tenets and practices. Islamic doctrines suggest that human destinies are not defined so much by individual actions as by divine will. Practicing Muslims commune with the divine spirit (Allah), praying five times each day, often in large groups of friends and strangers. Every year millions of people flock to Mecca to pay homage to Allah together.

• If you live in a densely populated place, maintaining group harmony becomes a key survival strategy. This might be one reason why a place like Japan evolved as a We-leaning culture, with millions of people needing to peacefully inhabit a group of very small islands.[17]

In contrast to this are more sparsely populated nations, like Canada, where self-reliance became essential for survival—and probably translated into a strong sense of individualism. Of course, there are places with low population densities that tend to be We leaning, and high-density Me-oriented nations that are more individualist. That's why all of these possible explanations are just considered theories.

As mentioned in chapter one, researchers in the field of cultural neuroscience even suggest that tendencies to be We- or Me-oriented have some genetic basis. In a study from Northwestern University conducted across 29 nations, researchers used brain scans to determine that people from We-oriented cultures are more likely to have a certain genetic marker (a form of the serotonin transporter gene, called the S-allele). [18]

Although the reasons for this genetic variation remain unclear, the study's authors (Joan Chiao and Katherine Blizinsky) offered up a few ideas. One of the theories described in their report suggests that this S-allele marker appears more often in We-oriented cultures as a result of a mix of genetic selection and environmental pressures and pathogens that have historically affected a region—like the prevalence of certain diseases. The idea is that some of the behaviors and values associated with being We oriented helped people survive the onslaught of diseases and pathogens, which in turn shaped the genetic selection of the population.[19] The researchers from Northwestern also explored the idea that this genetic marker associated with We cultures might correlate with higher rates of negative emotions, like anxiety and depression. After their studies revealed that people in We cultures were less likely to be depressed than those in Me cultures, the researchers concluded that collectivism may have co-evolved with the genetic marker in order to buffer people from depression. "In other words," explains a writer for the American Psychological Association, "societies of people with the S-allele developed a collectivist culture that reduced stress and, therefore, risk of depression by emphasizing social harmony and social support."[20]

Scientists and scholars will undoubtedly continue to study and debate the origins and physical manifestations of Me-We tendencies in the coming decades. While this is fascinating and important work, what's more relevant to most of us is the work we must do as individuals to become more aware of our own programming and consider how it impacts our behaviors, perceptions, and interpretations.

Whether we are talking about national, organizational, or any other kind of culture, Me-We programming has a profound and pervasive influence on everything from how we interact with others to how we perceive time—even how we design our homes. It shapes the way we see and respond to the world around us. Knowing where your Me-We tendencies lie is as important as knowing if you are near- or far-sighted: you can't adjust for a clearer view until you know your natural focal point.

ME VERSUS WE MARKETING

Consider some of the following slogans and how they may have been impacted by the Me-We orientation of the companies or the people to whom they are directed:

Me	We
I'm lovin' it! (McDonald's, United States)	**Everyone** loves McDonald's (Japan)
Can you hear me now? (Verizon, United States)	Have **all** freely connected (China Unicom)
Be all that **you** can be (Army, United States)	**Service before self** (Indian Army)
Where do **you** want to go today? (Microsoft)	**Everyone's** invited (Samsung, Korea)
iChat (Apple messaging service)	**WeChat** (Tencent, Chinese messaging service)

I'm not suggesting that the word "we" never show up in slogans targeting people from Me cultures, or that ads focused on individual gains never resonate with people who lean more toward the We side. Every culture has its own Me-We spin, making it difficult to predict what will hit the mark. Some cultures may even lean one way or the other depending on the kind of product that's being marketed.[21] But successful slogans can offer clues about a culture's tendencies or preferences—and if you are trying to sell something to a multicultural community, these slogans are a particularly valuable reminder to consider the Me-ness or We-ness of the consumers you are hoping to target.

CULTURE KEYS

Quick Tips for Me-We Crossings

MEETINGS

General Advice: To minimize crashes, send an agenda beforehand including the desired outcome of the meeting, discussion topics, list of presenters, and time limits.

With Me-oriented people	With We-oriented people
Share individual opinions and thoughts; this is valued and expected.	Give people time to check in with others before providing an answer.
Single people out for positive reasons; they will most likely appreciate this.	Avoid singling people out, whether for positive or negative reasons.
Get to the task quickly and don't feel slighted if no one lingers to chat.	Leave time for relationship building.

CONDUCTING INTERVIEWS

General Advice: Although these tips are for conducting interviews, if you are the interviewee, watch for these behavioral clues and adjust your behavior/responses to meet expectations.

With a Me-oriented person	With a We-oriented person
Keep in mind that candidates are expected to speak about individual achievements and play up leadership roles in group experiences.	Don't overlook someone because they don't focus on personal achievements; try to ask questions about experiences involving teamwork.

With a Me-oriented person	With a We-oriented person
Expect candidates to ask questions; this allows candidates to display their ability to think critically.	Don't expect candidates to ask too many questions; they may consider this poor form.
Expect candidates to freely and confidently share views and opinions as a sign of being confident.	Keep in mind that people may not feel it's appropriate to offer opinions or ideas during an interview; this does not mean they don't have them.

NETWORKING

In a Me culture	In a We culture
Expect people to make connections quickly and invite you to their online networks.	Be patient and show interest in and energy for a long-term relationship.
Be prepared for people to focus on their professional background versus personal.	Be prepared to engage in a series of reciprocal interactions to show dedication and build trust.
Don't be offended if people don't choose to socialize outside of work or stay only briefly when they do.	Dedicate time to socialize with people outside of the work/business environment. Meals and drinks can help solidify the relationship.

Say What?

Explore the nuances of verbal
and written expression

In the early '90s the California Milk Processor Board struck gold with their now classic "Got milk?" campaign. The campaign brilliantly captured the hearts of millions of people in the United States by making so many of us suddenly crave a glass of cool, creamy milk to wash down our cookies or loosen the peanut butter from the roof of our mouth.

The success of this ad prompted the Milk Board to expand the campaign to Latino consumers living in California. They did what most people with a basic grasp of Spanish language would do: they translated it as "*¿Tienes leche?*" Shortly after launching the Spanish language campaign, however, they discovered that "*¿Tienes leche?*" actually translates as "Are you lactating?" Not the kind of milk they had in mind.[1]

Translation blunders can range from funny to embarrassing to offensive. They can also lead to costly mistakes, like the one made by the Milk Board. Literal language differences are the most obvious barriers to verbal and written communication across cultures. With help from a dual language dictionary, differences in word choice and grammar become more navigable. But that dictionary will get you only so far.

Although the translations may seem clear, words and phrases are shape-shifters. Words can contain underlying meanings that are conveyed through a combination of nuances including tone, volume, and the context in which they're delivered. Timing and silence have implications too—implications that can vary widely between cultures.

Hidden messages embedded in the phrase "Got milk?" could have caused the advertisement to miss the mark with the Latino community even if the translation had been correct. While the idea of needing milk to wash down foods like cookies cleverly reminded many Americans to feed their "inner kid," researchers found that in some of California's Latino communities, where staples like milk are not always available or affordable, the question "Got milk?" evoked fears associated with not being able to feed your family. As a result, the advertisers modified their phrasing and strategy to target mothers and grandmothers who typically took pride in nourishing their families with milk-based products. The new tag line became "*¿Y usted les dio suficiente leche hoy?*" ("Have you given them enough milk today?"), and the ads highlighted traditional recipes that include milk, along with other imagery that evoked positive associations with food in that culture.[2]

When we communicate in our native tongue, we express hidden messages all the time without even realizing we are doing it. In a flash of a moment, we often subconsciously choose and deliver our words in specific ways in order to do things like present ourselves in a certain manner, elicit certain emotions, or protect others' feelings. In the context of our native cultures, we deftly wield these linguistic nuances to ensure that our intent matches our impact. Unfortunately, this same deep fluency can get us into trouble. With our brains on autopilot, we often assume that all of those implicit associations and meanings will be understood by others. But when we communicate across cultures, these hidden messages are often overlooked or misunderstood.

So how do we make sure that people aren't misinterpreting what we say? And on the flip side, how can we learn to "see" these hidden meanings and figure out what people from other cultures are really saying to us?

The good news is that there are clues that can help us decode the nuances of verbal communication—clues that become easier to detect and decipher after you've taken some time to size up your own communication style.

Are You Direct or Indirect?

A few months ago I gave a colleague a ride home from an evening event. We were deep in conversation as I started my car and pulled out of the parking lot into the dark night. My colleague realized that I had forgotten to turn on my lights and abruptly said, "Hey, you need to turn your lights on." I laughed at myself and said thanks as I flicked them on.

If the exact same situation happened but it was a Korean colleague instead of a U.S. native sitting next to me, the conversation might have unfolded a bit differently:

KOREAN COLLEAGUE: It's very dark outside tonight.

ME: Sure is.

KOREAN COLLEAGUE: But the stars light the road.

ME: Uh-huh. That's what stars do.

KOREAN COLLEAGUE: I wonder what else would light the road.

ME: Oh crap. Why didn't you just tell me to turn my lights on?

By the end of the conversation, I'm annoyed and my colleague is probably frustrated with me for taking so long to catch on. This shows how different verbal communication styles can lead to unnecessary conflict and emotional reactions. It also highlights one of the biggest distinctions between speaking styles across cultures: whether someone is a *direct* or an *indirect* communicator.

To better understand the distinction, think about what you would do if you were in the car with someone who has forgotten to turn on the headlights. Would you:

1. Quickly say, "Hey, turn your lights on."

2. Gently ask, "Did you turn your lights on yet?"

3. Casually note, "It's very dark outside tonight, isn't it?"

If you are someone who appreciates the "tell it to me straight" approach, you probably picked 1. If you prefer a slightly less direct manner, 2 is clearly a better option. And for those sensitive to embarrassment and mood disruption, option 3 should do the trick.

We each have our own personal preferences when it comes to being direct or indirect, but culture also plays a significant role. If you come from a national, regional, or even organizational culture that places a high value on saving face, for example, you are more likely to use an indirect communication style, like the Korean colleague in the scenario just described. Social scientists refer to cultures in which people tend to express themselves indirectly as *high context*, meaning that there is a heavy reliance on contextual clues to communicate, like carefully choosing words to avoid losing face or expressing respect and rank through eye contact. Indirect comments are often carefully and strategically crafted to minimize embarrassment and offensiveness. Questions, requests, and responses are framed to save face in ways that may seem unnecessary to someone from another culture, as in letting someone know that they've forgotten to turn their headlights on.

On the other end of the spectrum are *low-context* cultures, in which communication is more explicit and speaking styles are more *direct*, with few contextual clues required. In low-context cultures, words can often be taken at face value and there's relatively less need to read meaning into contextual cues (including nonverbal cues, which we will explore in the next chapter).

Whether people tend to be direct or indirect when they communicate is only part of what qualifies a culture as high or low context—but in my experience, it's the one that creates the most challenges. Daily occurrences at work—like making requests, running meetings, delivering feedback, and setting expectations—are potential pitfalls if the people interacting are accustomed to different levels of directness.

One of the most confusing and frustrating crash points has to do with the seemingly simple act of saying "no." In cultures that tend more toward indirect communication, people are more likely to avoid saying no if possible. Instead, they say yes even when they mean no, or they do a verbal dance to avoid giving a definitive answer. It might go something like this:

Q: Can you work with Harper to plan the community event for next week?

A: The next event is very soon. Harper is good at planning them—much better than I am.

The responder might have been implying either that they were too busy to do it now, or that they didn't like working with Harper. People on the receiving end of this kind of indirect framing are supposed to read between the lines. The problem is, if someone comes from a culture where direct responses are expected, they are likely to take the words at face value and miss the true message.

An interior designer I know encountered this kind of communication crash while working with a group of Mexican architects. Several times the designer (a U.S. native) asked them to deliver a specific style of drawing. They always said yes, but they would never deliver. After weeks of frustration, it finally occurred to him that the architects were saying no without saying no. Perhaps they didn't have the capacity to produce these kinds of drawings or simply didn't think they were necessary. In other situations, the architects were fairly direct with him about their opinions and ideas, so it didn't occur to him that they wouldn't be up front about this.

His story underscores an important point about verbal communication styles: they change depending on the context. No matter what culture you hail from, chances are you range between direct and indirect, depending on the situation: softening your commentary to preserve face in some situations, being more direct in others. Knowing when to be direct or indirect is an essential and highly nuanced facet of communication that can vary widely among national, regional, workplace, and community cultures. The nuances are partly based on personal style and largely based on cultural programming and expectations.

To get a better sense of whether you tend more toward directness or indirectness, scan the following lists of behavioral patterns. Put a checkmark (actual or mental) next to your general preferences and see if your tendencies align more with the descriptions in column A (Direct) or column B (Indirect).

A: As a *direct* person, you tend to:	B: As an *indirect* person, you tend to:
☐ Strive to express yourself clearly via verbal communication whenever possible, and expect to receive information in a similar manner.	☐ Rely heavily on nonverbal cues like silent pauses and gestures to convey meanings, and assume others will do the same.
☐ Immediately speak to the task at hand and minimize time spent talking about irrelevant topics.	☐ Before talking about tasks, try to make time to talk about other topics to cultivate the relationship.
☐ Generally believe that speaking plainly and truthfully is the best course, even if it may disappoint or upset the other person.	☐ Generally believe that the preservation of positive feelings and harmony outweigh the importance of being clear, direct and truthful.

A: As a *direct* person, you tend to:	B: As an *indirect* person, you tend to:
☐ Assume that no means no and yes means yes.	☐ Avoid saying no whenever possible, and say maybe or yes even when you mean no.

Despite the variables—and even if your tendencies are split evenly down the middle—this chart offers a good way to fix the "true north" on your personal communication compass. In turn, this will help you with the next step: recognizing your perceptions of directness and indirectness in various scenarios—and adjusting your reactions to yield better results.

Assertive, Aggressive, or Passive: Recognizing Perceptions and Adjusting Reactions

The fact that the same words can be interpreted very differently across cultures can be problematic on multiple levels, but it's how we react to these interpretations that can really lead to big trouble. The way that we outwardly respond to our interpretations can lead to a culture crash—or enable us to avert one. For example, if I'm from a culture that tends toward a more direct communication style, I may become annoyed if someone isn't more direct with me, as I did in that scenario in which my Korean colleague indirectly told me to turn on my headlights. I would be frustrated by a perceived waste of time or perceive the speaker as lacking confidence or behaving suspiciously. My negative reactions would be reflected in what I say, my tone, and my body language. Conversely, someone from a culture where people tend to be relatively indirect communicators might have a negative reaction to someone else's more direct style of speaking. Their outward responses might reflect their perception of the speaker's blunt style as being rude, disrespectful, or thoughtless.

One way to reduce the likelihood of these kinds of crashes is to *recognize* when something someone said or wrote makes you feel confused, surprised, or annoyed—then hit your personal pause button and consider whether you might be in the midst of a direct-indirect crash. It may take a few seconds or even a few minutes, but once you *open your mind* to the idea that you might be misinterpreting what someone is saying, you can *adjust your reaction* to avoid harming the relationship. In the headlight scenario, if I had been more attuned to differences in communication styles I might have recognized that I was perplexed by my Korean colleague's starlight ruminations. In turn, this would've prompted me to consider if he was trying to communicate something indirectly, perhaps to save me from embarrassment. Bearing in mind the "why" behind his words, instead of voicing my aggravation I would have been more likely to switch on my lights with a quick smile, acknowledging his hint. This would have avoided frustration and saved face, and maybe even saved me from driving into the bushes.

Culture crashes between indirect and direct communicators can occur in countless situations, but the crashes can be particularly tense when it comes to giving and receiving feedback. We give and receive feedback in every aspect of our lives, from offering an opinion about a business plan or a piece of art to admiring a new haircut. Everybody has their own way of doing it, but culture often plays a role.

I'm frequently called upon to help people avoid feedback crashes at U.S.-based companies that have hired international staff to work in U.S.-based headquarters—or have set up satellite offices in other countries. In one instance, an American employee was dumbfounded by the negative feedback she received from a Dutch colleague, who told her in no uncertain terms that her work was subpar and unacceptable. It went something like this:

> Your report is not good enough. Your data is weak. Work on it and send it to me again.

As a result, the American employee reached out to human resources to lodge a complaint about her Dutch colleague's aggressive communication style. The Dutch colleague was totally shocked by this reaction, because in her mind, she was just giving feedback in a professional way. It was by no means intended as a personal attack.

People from the United States often think of themselves as direct, but in truth, there are a number of other cultures in which people tend to be even more direct. In general, we cannot accurately judge our own degree of directness or indirectness until we experience other behaviors that provide a point of reference. Think about how you prefer to give and receive feedback about a report. How would you have perceived that negative feedback from the Dutch colleague—as aggressive or assertive? Would it have been more acceptable to you if she had offered feedback like this?

> The report you submitted is a good start. There are some things that you need to develop further, but otherwise it seems fine. Keep up the good work!

Or maybe you are accustomed to an even more indirect and face-saving style, like this:

> The graphics in the report were very well done. Do you think we should proceed with the data as is?

Or would you think that response was too vague and passive? Not unlike Goldilocks trying out the three chairs (too hard, too soft, or just right), we each have our own comfort zones when it comes to receiving and giving feedback and other forms of verbal communication. Social psychologists have boiled down our interpretations of different communication styles into three main categories: passive, aggressive, or assertive. Most people think of passive and aggressive as negative qualities, while being assertive is viewed as a positive behavior. The catch is that what one person perceives as assertive, another may perceive as aggressive or passive, and vice versa.

Thankfully, it's possible to detect these differences in intention. For example, the U.S. American employee could have noted how irritated she was by the email, and then paused to consider if the Dutch colleague had previously sent positive emails in a similarly blunt tone. If so, that would suggest this was just her normal way of communicating and there was no need to be offended. If the U.S. American was not able to adjust her emotional response to the direct tone, however, another option would be to have an open discussion with the Dutch colleague, letting her know how her emails were being perceived. Although it may not resolve the issue completely, with better awareness on both sides communication usually improves.

The way that differing perceptions of aggressive, assertive, and passive behavior play out along cultural lines is particularly notable when comparing Japanese and U.S. culture. I recently flew to Tokyo to work with a Japanese division of a well-known U.S. tech company. The company had hired me to help train the Japanese employees to be more assertive. The problem was that the U.S. American staff members perceived their Japanese counterparts as passive and disengaged, largely because the Japanese coworkers didn't speak up enough in meetings and didn't offer their opinions or provide direct responses—all behaviors that the U.S. Americans equate with assertiveness.

When I talked to the Japanese employees, however, they didn't see themselves as passive at all. They actually perceived the U.S. Americans as aggressive for being so direct in their feedback style, and because they never stopped talking long enough for any of the Japanese to enter the conversation. Many Japanese are programmed from childhood to not interrupt others who are talking (that would be considered aggressive), so it's little wonder that they would have trouble jumping into the conversation and that they might perceive the U.S. American's interruptions as rude and aggressive.

During my time with the Japanese staff, I made them aware of all these misperceptions, and I had them practice being more assertive as defined by their U.S. American colleagues. Overriding their cultural instincts will be no small feat, but with practice it will become easier and will surely build mutual confidence among team members from the two different cultures, ultimately leading to greater overall effectiveness and productivity.

Any time we interact with someone from another culture, we are prone to apply labels like aggressive, assertive, or passive based on varying levels of directness and indirectness. Our minds unconsciously apply these labels in countless other aspects of our lives too, causing us to make judgments based on misinterpreted information. Of course, this also means that people are making assumptions about *us* and what *we* are trying to communicate based on misinterpreted information.

Adding to the complexity, our perception of a particular communication style can change depending on the situation. For example, think about your expectations when you go shopping for large household electronics, like a television. Do you expect the salesperson to approach you, ask questions, and offer advice? Would you see this as assertive or aggressive behavior? But what if you were shopping for food in a large grocery store and a salesperson acted the same way. Does your expectation or perception change depending on what you're buying?

Whether shopping, getting feedback from a colleague, negotiating a business deal, bargaining at a market, or simply chatting with a friend, if we think someone is being aggressive it can automatically send us into flight-or-fight mode. Conversely, when we perceive someone as being assertive, our brain usually engages in a positive way. I am much more likely to buy something from a salesperson who meets my personal definition of assertive. In my case, this includes asking if I need assistance (but only once) and answering my questions in a confident, friendly, and prompt manner. For others, their definition of assertive may include either less or more communication. For some, friendliness may not be required, while for others, being assertive may entail having an extended conversation that has nothing to do with the potential purchase.

There is no right or wrong when it comes to your perceptions of aggressive, assertive, or passive communication styles. Similarly, while you might think of being direct or indirect as having advantages or shortcomings in certain situations, the point is not to judge the merits of each, but to understand that they can easily lead to a culture crash if we don't consider how we might misinterpret the words we hear (or don't hear)—or how *our* words may be misinterpreted. Once our minds are open to this, we can detect the clues and adjust our reactions accordingly.

For example, if my intent is to be direct and assertive but I notice people backing away or acting defensive, they might perceive me as aggressive. This is my cue to try softening my tone and volume. If my intent is to be assertive, but I sense that people are not paying attention or not including me in the discussion, they might perceive me as being passive. In this instance, I would try shifting my style by speaking with more volume, speaking more succinctly, or simply speaking up. There's no failsafe method of ensuring that people will understand your intentions, but you'll increase the odds by looking for clues like these and tweaking your communication style until the response feels right.

It can be particularly challenging—and frustrating—to adjust for assertiveness if you are a woman. There is a tendency in many cultures to view a woman's communication style as more aggressive than if a man had delivered the message in the exact same way. It's a classic double standard that is often worsened when cultural differences are thrown into the mix. Also, men may feel that they can be more or less direct when communicating with women than with men, depending on the situation. Whether you are male or female, communication across genders can be complex and fraught with both conscious and unconscious biases. It's up to each of us to size up the interaction, consider the cultural programming of the man or woman with whom we are interacting, and decide how—or if—we want to proceed with the communication.

Communication Style by Country

Nineteen-year-old Edward T. Hall began his career the same way that most other cultural anthropologists did in the first half of the twentieth century: by immersing himself in the study of singular cultures. From 1933 through 1937, Hall lived and worked with the Navajo and the Hopi on Native American reservations in Arizona.[3] As his career evolved over the years, so too did his vision for a new approach to cultural anthropology. Instead of studying single cultures or comparing entire cultures to each other, Hall began to focus on the interactions between people of different cultures, and in doing so laid the foundation for this fascinating field of study to which I've dedicated my career.

One of the catalysts for this new focus came as a result of Hall's stint at the U.S. State Department in the 1950s, where he taught intercultural communications skills to foreign-service staff. By addressing the issues and needs of his students, Hall began amassing a body of research related to points of divergence between cultures. As his work continued into the 1960s and '70s, he introduced a number of concepts related to intercultural relations that formed the basis of future work by cross-cultural scholars and educators around the globe.[4]

One of Hall's most widely known concepts is the notion of high context and low context[5] that I mentioned earlier in the chapter. But also notable—and useful—is that Hall plotted the results of his studies along a spectrum, which can be used to help anticipate if people are more likely to be direct or indirect communicators. Although he plotted his results more than four decades ago, subsequent studies have upheld most of his findings. Many recent studies have also translated the notion of high and low context into more user-friendly and specific terms, creating spin-off spectrums that relate to things like tolerance for silence and being indirect versus direct.

One of the more comprehensive direct-indirect studies was conducted by The Brannen Group, a global cross-cultural consulting firm. In the study, which involved over two hundred thousand participants from around the globe, people were given a series of questions to answer related to their communication preferences in a variety of situations. The results were ranked on a scale from 1 to 100, with the lowest number being the most indirect and the highest the most direct. Figure 3.1 shows a sample of how some countries are ranked when plotted along a spectrum.

It's important to note that these rankings reflect the way people tend to communicate during the initial stages of relationship building. As Brannen Group CEO Chris Brannen explained to me in an email:

> This is because many cultures that rank on the indirect end of the communication dimension can often become surprisingly direct once the business relationship is established. As a notable example of this shift, Japanese, in general, are initially indirect in communications. However, when two negotiating parties are no longer strangers and the business relationship has become established, the Japanese cultural norm can switch rather dramatically to the direct end of the communication dimension. A similar switch from an indirect to a direct communication style can also occur in other cultures, for example, the Middle East, China, and Spain.

Of course, not everyone from a certain culture will demonstrate the same degree of directness or indirectness when building relationships, partly because the individual's personality and preferences

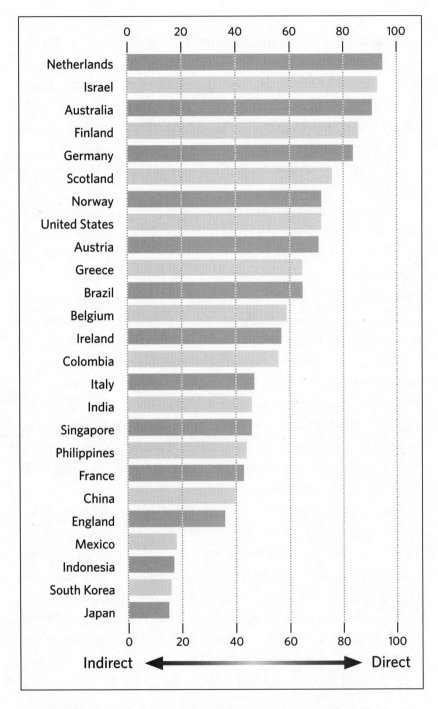

Figure 3.1: Country styles on the Indirect-Direct continuum. Data from The Brannen Group.

always play a role. Some people may be indirect when it comes to giving bad news, for example, but they may communicate in a much more direct way when giving feedback. The spectrum does show that certain countries lean more toward direct or indirect communication styles—tendencies that often ring true, in my experience. Identifying tendencies is a great way to start figuring people out, as long as we remember that there are always exceptions. It also helps you gauge whether your own tendencies are right in line with those of your home culture, or not.

The same kind of spectrum can be created for regional differences, often reflecting varying levels of directness among people in northern, southern, eastern, and western areas of a single country. You can also chart the communication style of organizations, including companies, non-profit ventures, government, educational institutions, and so on. Through my work in Silicon Valley, I've witnessed surprisingly stark differences in how people tend to communicate at tech companies like Google, Apple, Uber, and Evernote. Some of these business cultures encourage more indirect communication styles among their staff as a means of maintaining a strong sense of camaraderie and harmony. In other places, employees and consultants are expected to be vocal and to the point about opinions that can advance the company's goals. There tends to be little sugarcoating because there's less emphasis on maintaining group harmony.

From start-up cupcake shops to nationwide legal firms to global health institutes, each group cultivates its own way of communicating. When you start working with any organization, it's essential to get familiar with expectations for levels of directness in various situations, particularly for giving and receiving feedback, making requests, engaging in small talk, and voicing displeasure. You will undoubtedly find greater success if you check your assumptions at the door, take time to observe how people interact in the organization, and consider if you need to modify your personal communication style and perceptions.

When There Are No Words: Silence

In my house, the chatter is fairly constant. When I go out with friends in my neighborhood, there's rarely a gap of more than a few seconds before someone feels compelled to say something. Same goes for business negotiations. When it's quiet in the car for more than five seconds, my young daughter asks: "What's wrong?"

I didn't realize how uncomfortable I was with silence in conversations until I began working in places where people *were* comfortable with silence. Over the years I've become more at ease with silence, but it can still feel awkward, largely because I was programmed to feel that way from a very young age.

When kids in the United States misbehave, they're often given a time-out, which usually means that they have to stay in part of a room by themselves and are forbidden to make a noise or converse with anyone else. When they have successfully completed their silent time, they are allowed to return to the land of noise. The message is quite clear to most kids: Silence equals punishment. Talking equals reward. Later in life people are introduced to the "silent treatment" as a means of expressing displeasure with someone. Nothing makes me beg forgiveness faster than this close-lipped type of communication. For me and most other U.S. natives, silence creates a strong sense of discomfort and often signals that someone is unhappy with us.

There's an experiment that I like to do in my workshops in which I pause after completing a thought, as if I'm contemplating my next statement. But instead of taking a one- to two-second pause, I remain silent for about five to seven seconds—and I observe what happens with my audience. In the United States, the majority of the audience starts to cough, laugh, talk to themselves out loud, and get wiggly in their seats right around the three-second mark. The signs of discomfort just increase as the time passes. Afterward, I ask the audience how my silence made them feel. For many, it's excruciatingly awkward.

It's an unexpected occurrence that makes people assume there is a problem. Participants tell me that they think that I forgot what I was about to say, I'm not feeling well, or I had a sudden and urgent realization—like leaving the stove on in my house or having missed my mother's birthday.

Next I ask participants to extrapolate: "What is your gut reaction when a question you ask is met with silence, whether it be by a colleague, customer, friend, or family member?" People native to the United States generally assume that their question wasn't understood by the listener, or that the listener didn't know the answer or simply didn't like the question. They tend to see silence as a negative.

When I put this question to people from other cultures, however, they may tell me that their first interpretation of the silence is to assume the listener is thinking, taking time to formulate a thoughtful and accurate response to the question. In their way of communicating, longer silences are expected and appreciated. People from these cultures don't get wiggly until about the seven-second mark, if at all. I recently asked a group of Japanese people participating in my workshop what they thought might be their tolerance for an extended silence during a conversation, and their response was "About thirty seconds."

In just the same way that I was programmed early in life to associate silence with negativity, people from other cultures may have been programmed to associate silence with positive attributes like thoughtful consideration and harmony.

In many cultures, kids are conditioned from an early age to tolerate silences of five seconds or more—what others would consider prolonged. A client of mine from Finland recalls being taught from a young age not to rush into responses; to take time to contemplate questions and respond thoughtfully. She explained to me that during conversations, there are very few "Uh-huhs," "Yeps," "Hmmms," or other silence fillers needed to indicate that a person is still listening or thinking. She said that silences are perceived as treasured moments and signs of respect, and they are expected in all forms of conversation.

Programming around silence is also reflected and reinforced through religion. In countries where Buddhism is dominant—like Thailand, Myanmar, and Japan, for example—people practice their religion by sitting in a silent meditative state, sometimes for hours on end. Emphasis is placed on quieting all internal dialogue in an effort to achieve a higher state of consciousness. Silence is an essential part of the path to enlightenment.

On the extreme opposite end of the sound spectrum are certain Christian denominations in the United States, in which loud songs and fervent oratory characterize the spiritual path. During the Sunday sermons at Glide Memorial Church in San Francisco, the reverend frequently and purposefully gets louder and louder as he builds up to the climax of his sermon. The congregation responds to any pauses with equal gusto, issuing a thunderous "Amen" at the appropriate points. As the sermon reaches a crescendo, the music begins and everybody starts singing, clapping, and stomping their feet, creating a surge of sound intended to bring everyone closer to touching the divine.

Comparing this to the Buddhist way represents two ends of the spectrum, but every religion uses sound in different ways—ways that seep into our subconscious, shaping our perceptions of silence. Over the years I have seen opposing perceptions of silence lead to unfortunate cross-cultural misunderstandings. One arena in which silence can really wreak havoc is the dreaded global conference call, whether people on either end of the call are actually abroad or just from different cultural backgrounds. Maybe this scenario will sound familiar to you:

YOU: Can we get a status update?

THEM: *A few seconds of silence*

YOU: Did you get that? I asked for an update? Can you hear me?

THEM: *More silence*

YOU: Hello? Are you guys there?
(*Nervously looking at others in the room*)

Barring technical and translation problems, another common explanation is that the people on the other end of the line are simply thinking about the question, gathering consensus, or trying to figure out how to thoughtfully answer the question or minimize any loss of face.

Whether on a call like this or in person, it can be hard to keep our kneejerk responses at bay. But in truth, it's easily navigated just by having some patience. I often suggest that my clients allow seven seconds before starting to ask follow-up questions. Those seven seconds may seem like an eternity to some, but patience usually pays off. Seven seconds allows time for people to process the question, translate it into their native language and then back again if needed, build consensus, and then formulate a well-thought-out response. If you put yourself in their shoes and consider all that needs to be accomplished, even seven seconds starts to feel inadequate.

Conversely, if you're talking with people who are uncomfortable with silence, it's best to respond promptly if possible. Even if you don't have an immediate answer, you can always let them know you need a few seconds to respond. Chances are they won't mind waiting a few more seconds. A simple "Yes," "Got it," or "Let me think about it for a moment" is an easy way to acknowledge that you are engaged, and can go a long way toward easing the minds of others who are wary of silence.

Whether communicating with someone virtually or face to face, your best bet for figuring out if that person perceives silence as a positive or negative is to recognize how the silence is making you feel, then consider some of the other ways of perceiving silence that we've discussed in this chapter, and finally, adjust your response and see how it plays out.

Reminding yourself of your own comfort level with silence even before the meeting starts could enable you to head off feelings of unease or aggravation even more quickly. How long is too long to be silent? When do you get wiggly? Test it out with a friend and consider what silence means to you. Only after you do that can you truly start to open your mind to different ways of perceiving silence. Of course, silence is only the tip of the iceberg when it comes to communicating without words, which is why we will spend the next chapter exploring how other forms of nonverbal communication are used and perceived in ways that you—or anyone—may be barely aware of.

CULTURE KEY

Quick Tips for Direct-Indirect Crossings

	For Direct communicators interacting with more indirect people:	For Indirect communicators interacting with more direct people:
During conversations and meetings:	If it takes a while for the person to get to the point, try to be patient. That person may place more emphasis on building relationships than on completing tasks in that context.	Communicating your message quickly and succinctly is generally expected and appreciated. Wait too long, and the person may lose interest or become nervous.
Disagreeing and giving feedback:	Avoid outright disagreement if possible to avoid incurring a loss of face. If the feedback is negative, find ways to soften your words and put a more positive spin on them.	Disagreement is not generally perceived as a personal affront. When giving feedback, use words to articulate your true feelings, intentions, and expectations. Being direct and explicit is often appreciated and seen as a positive quality.

	For Direct communicators interacting with more indirect people:	For Indirect communicators interacting with more direct people:
Responding to requests:	Watch for people implying "no" without actually saying "No." Signs of "no" may include fillers like "Hmm," repeating the question, or sucking air between teeth; angling or scratching their head; an abrupt change of subject; even a smile. Use these same strategies to imply "no" without offending someone.	It's okay to just say "No." Don't be offended if someone denies your request outright.

General Advice: Avoid sarcasm, which can easily be misinterpreted across cultures.

FOUR

What's Not Being Said

Discover the hidden meanings
of nonverbal communication

What's a gesture that means the same thing in every culture? Any guesses? I've asked this same question of over twelve thousand people from about fifty countries. I define gesture here in the broadest sense, as a movement of part of the body to express an idea or meaning, without words.

One of the most popular answers to my question is "Nodding to say 'Yes' or shaking your head left-right to mean 'No.'" Other common responses include the middle finger, the okay sign, and thumbs up. See Figure 4.1 for illustrations.

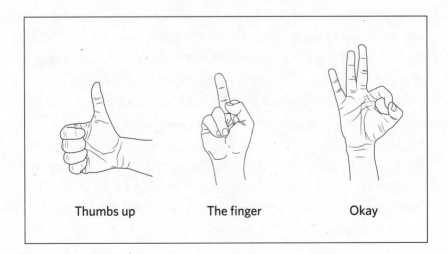

| Thumbs up | The finger | Okay |

Figure 4.1: Hand gestures

People are often surprised when I tell them that those answers are all wrong. In fact, I've yet to find any gesture that means the same thing no matter where you are in the world. I almost always ask this question at the start of my workshops as a way of introducing the idea that it's not safe to assume that any gesture means the same thing across cultures. This includes dozens of common gestures, such as how we point, how we beckon someone to approach us or tell them to go away, how we hold our arms when talking, and so on.

As mentioned earlier in the book, Microsoft founder Bill Gates learned how even the simplest gesture can be misconstrued during a trip to South Korea, where he met with president Park Geun-hye. Press photographers snapped photos of Gates shaking hands with the president with his left hand stuffed in his pocket. The next day in Korea's leading newspaper, *JoongAng Ilbo*, the headline read "Cultural difference, or an act of disrespect?" Another newspaper ran with "Disrespectful handshake? Casual handshake?" next to the photo.[1] Mr. Gates clearly didn't know that the proper greeting to someone of high status in South Korea is to use two hands clasped around their one. Keeping your hand in your pants pocket while shaking with the other one is considered disrespectful.

Although this faux pas merely created some bad press for Mr. Gates, using the wrong gesture could theoretically lead to dire consequences—as it did in the Quentin Tarantino movie *Inglourious Basterds*. Set in Nazi-occupied France during World War II, the film follows a group of Jewish soldiers on a mission to assassinate Nazi leaders. At one point, a British lieutenant impersonates a high-ranking Nazi officer at a gathering in a pub with other German soldiers. His German is fluent, his knowledge of German culture seemingly perfect. Things are going just fine until the Brit signals the bartender to order another round of beers for the three men sitting at the table. Moments later the Germans start shooting at him and everyone else in the pub.

What happened?

The Nazi officers in this movie picked up on the difference in how British and German people count on their fingers. The typical German hand sign for the number three is thumb, index, and middle fingers, but he unthinkingly used the English sign, in which the first three fingers are used, not the thumb (see Figure 4.2).

Of course, in real life, indicating a number is unlikely to get you into trouble, but there are plenty of other gestures that can. And what about other ways that we communicate without words? When you think about nonverbal communication, the first thing that comes to mind are hand and head gestures like the ones just noted, but there's much more to it than that. Nonverbal communication also encompasses things like how far apart you stand from someone, the amount of eye contact you use, how you greet someone, and even how you position your feet. I've learned over the years that something as habitual and seemingly innocuous as scratching your head, running your fingers under your chin, tapping your foot, or rolling your eyes may put you at risk of miscommunication without your ever uttering a word.

So what do we do? Keep our arms and hands glued to the side of our bodies, eyes closed, and feet on the floor at all times so as not to

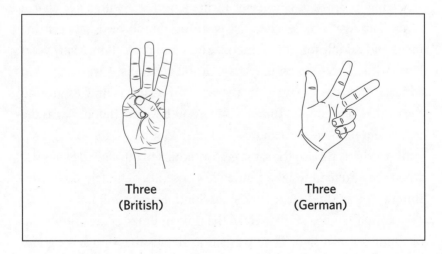

Three
(British)

Three
(German)

Figure 4.2: Hand gestures

offend anybody? Memorize every gesture ever used? Clearly that's not possible. Thankfully, it's also unnecessary. In this chapter we depart from our more general approach of surveying cross-cultural differences and delve into specific nonverbal gestures that are most likely to get you into trouble. Simply becoming familiar with this set of gestures—including the set of personal gestures that you probably use without conscious effort—will give you a head start when it comes to avoiding a culture crash. In lieu of taking a self-assessment quiz, I suggest activities you can do later to observe your nonverbal behaviors in action.

Reading the Signs

Gestures are among the first behaviors we learn in life. Parents and caregivers smile at newborns and shake their heads yes and no in certain ways. Gestures that are learned early in life become second nature and deeply engrained in our unconscious communication style. As we grow up, countless other gestures and nonverbal nuances become part of an unspoken lexicon, a veritable language that we often forget to "translate" when communicating with people from other cultures.

Living in Brazil as a teenager I wore a necklace with a *figa* charm on it. The figa is a clenched fist with the thumb held between the index and middle finger to symbolize luck and protection. Many years later, while I was studying cross-cultural relations, I was surprised to learn that the Brazilian figa is used by many countries around the world (for example, Turkey, China, South Korea, Indonesia) as the equivalent to the American middle finger. Good luck for some, "F*** you" to others. It's also the same gesture adults in the United States use when they pretend to take a little kid's nose. It's definitely not something you want to do to a Turkish or South Korean child.

Another hand gesture used all the time in Brazil is the thumbs-up or thumbs-down sign. The up position signals that things are good; down implies not good. In the United States the sign is used similarly, and is also used in the "up" position to hitch a ride. In many parts of Greece, Australia, and the Middle East, however, a thumbs-up sign can be construed as "up yours" and probably won't get you a ride in the right direction.

The U.S. "okay" sign, the circled thumb and index finger, can also cause problems. Brazilians use an inverted okay sign in a very crude way to tell someone to f*** off. In France it means "zero" or "worthless." In Japan it may mean "Give me money" in certain contexts, while in Colombia, if you hold the okay sign up to your nose it's a derogatory way to suggest someone is homosexual.

Besides sanctioned gestures like the thumbs-up and okay signs, there are also a wide variety of meaningless "filler" gestures that we all use—the equivalent of a verbal "um." My father taps his belly, my daughter twitches her nose, and I often rub the side of my face when conversing. These fillers and other types of habitual movements may seem innocuous, but they could easily be misinterpreted.

For example, imagine you're at a meeting and the person running it starts off by standing up with his hands placed on his hips. What does this "hands on hips" body language suggest to you? Does it suggest power and confidence—or maybe arrogance or aggressiveness? Does it say I am happy, full of energy, and ready to go (à la Peter Pan)? Sometimes when people put their hands on their hips it's simply a place to rest their hands because they don't know what else to do with them, but how would anyone know this? They can only make inferences based on their cultural upbringing. That's why it's important to be aware that the intention (or lack of intention) behind your gesture may not have the desired effect.

The first step in minimizing this kind of gesture misinterpretation is to take stock of the gestures you use regularly and try not to use them in multicultural settings. Think about the hand gestures you use most often. What about facial gestures? Do you roll your eyes? Are you a winker? What do you do with your legs when you are sitting? Most of us don't even know what we do. When I ask people in my workshops to name their top three most frequently used gestures, they are usually stumped, underscoring how unaware we can be of our own bodies.

During one of my workshops in Texas, a salesperson recognized his tendency to lick his lips while conversing with people, and that his lip licking may have botched a sale. He recalls being in the stages of closing a large deal, when the buyer paused and scrutinized the seller's face and then abruptly called the whole thing off. Although it's hard to know exactly why he walked away, the salesperson's assessment was that the lip licking could have suggested to the buyer that he was being manipulated or taken advantage of. Through this simple act, the salesperson may have inadvertently cast himself in the role of a hungry wolf in anticipation of the kill.

Armed with this new self-awareness, the salesman will be better able to stop himself from licking his lips during any kind of negotiation. Similarly, you'll be able to put the brakes on your own default gestures once you've identified them. A good way to identify your gestures is to ask others what they observe about you, especially people with whom you spend a lot of time, like family members and close friends. You could even have somebody make a video of you while you are having a conversation or conducting a meeting.

Recognizing your own gestures is the first step to being able to modify them, and to avoid a potential culture crash. The next step is to get familiar with some other common gestures and forms of wordless communication that are most likely to lead to misunderstandings.

Come Here!

When you want someone to come with or toward you, chances are you use your hand to signal it. But there are a surprising number of variations of this beckoning motion across cultures, and if you use the wrong one, you could be not only misunderstood, but also perceived as disrespectful.

In the United States, most parts of Europe, and Australia, people tend to beckon with their palm facing up, toward their chest. But in many other cultures—such as China, Japan, Saudi Arabia, and Thailand—the palm is face down, with the fingers making a scratching motion toward the palm. Beckoning with a palm up in some of these cultures can be construed as belittling or threatening. Watch any old kung-fu movie, and you are likely to see one fighter challenging the other by beckoning with the palm up as if to say, "Bring it!" In South Korea, the palm-up version tends to be used for calling animals, so you can imagine the implication if you were to do this to a person.

In places where palm up is the norm like the United States, gesturing with the palm down is used only for small children (and only occasionally). The implications aren't overly negative, but you might get some strange looks. There is also the single finger method of beckoning, which can have different meanings depending on the context. In the Philippines and Mexico, for example, summoning someone with one finger is considered suitable only for animals and can be perceived as insulting if directed to a person. In many cultures the single finger is used to call little children in an affectionate manner, while in other cultures it's used mostly to imply a sexual advance.

My suggestion is to avoid all nonverbal beckoning unless you are 100-percent sure of how it may be interpreted.

What's the Point?

In the United States, most people point with their index finger or pointer finger, as it's aptly called. Finger pointing is used no matter whether someone is pointing to another a person, to an object, or in a direction. In many cultures, however, using your finger to point at others is considered impolite or downright rude. In some cultures the index finger is used for pointing at objects, but never at people.

There are plenty of other ways to point, too. In Brazil many people use their chins to point, and in certain parts of West Africa the elbow is used. In the Dominican Republic, Cuba, and Puerto Rico people often point by puckering their lips combined with a slight tilt of the head, a gesture that avoids finger pointing, but could suggest a sexual come-on in the United States.

Your best chance for avoiding an offense in any culture is simply to do what people in countries like Japan, Vietnam, and Bahrain do: point using an open hand. Although the open hand could have some implications in certain cultures, experts generally agree that it's the safest bet.

Yes and No

In most cultures, nodding your head up and down means "yes" and shaking it side to side means "no." As noted in the introduction, Bulgaria is one of the few places where the signs are reversed: shaking your head from side to side indicates "yes" and an up-and-down movement means "no." This habit is insanely hard for anyone to break, in terms of both how we perceive the signs and getting our brains to reverse our way of responding. Give it a try if you haven't already.

Most of us rarely have to contend with the full reversal of yes and no signs; we're more likely to encounter (and have trouble with) the head wobble. This side-to-side movement of the head, which can mean "maybe" in the United States and other places, usually means, "Yes, I understand" or "I agree" in many parts of India, Sri Lanka, and Bangladesh.

Over the years many of my participants have relayed stories in which they misinterpreted head wobbles as a "maybe" or a "no." They eventually figured out that it was equivalent to a "yes" nod used to indicate understanding and agreement, but not before suffering through a period of confusion and frustration. If you are unclear about the meaning of a head movement or any other nonverbal implication of yes or no, it's always best to use words to confirm.

Count with Caution

A German friend of mine began frequenting a local juice shop shortly after moving from Germany to Southern California. Each morning she would order two juices, one for her and another for her coworker. To indicate that she wanted two juices, she used her thumb and index finger (making an L shape) to signal the number two. Every time she did this, the twenty-year-olds behind the counter at the juice shop seemed perplexed. They heard her say "two," but her gesture looked to them like she was saying one. A few months later she also learned that the German sign for the number two can be used to signify "loser" in the United States.

The fact that people use different fingers for counting generally doesn't cause problems (except if you are a foreign spy in a Quentin Tarantino movie), but it's worth noting because different finger configurations can actually imply other meanings, and even different numbers. For example, raising your thumb, index, and middle finger all at once is a gesture connected to Serbian nationalism. So if you are interacting with Serbians, you might want to use other fingers. In the United States, U.K., and Australia, people signal the number five by extending all five fingers, palm facing out. In Greece, this gesture is called the *moutza* and is very offensive (often defined as "I throw poop in your face"). For this reason, Greeks are careful not to fully extend their hand when counting the number five on their fingers. The moutza is also used in Pakistan and some African nations.

In Japan, people don't have to worry about their five fingers being mistaken for a moutza because they often indicate the number five with a closed fist. But they should be concerned that this closed fist might signal to someone in the United States a sign of power or solidarity, or that the gesturer wants to fight. The likelihood of misunderstanding a number count is even greater in other parts of Asia, where people count to twelve using a single hand (they include finger bones or knuckles), and you may wind up with way more than you thought you bargained for.[2]

Behind the Smile

Although facial expressions like the smile are not technically gestures, I'm including the smile here because so many people think it is universally understood. But it's not. The messages behind the smile—or lack of a smile—are often misunderstood when people cross cultures.

Social scientists had long believed that smiling is an inborn and universal motor routine triggered by a feeling of happiness.[3] This theory dates all the way back to 1872, when naturalist Charles Darwin first made this assertion in his book *The Expression of the Emotions in Man and Animals*. But recent studies suggest that the way we express and perceive a smile and other emotional expressions is largely defined by our cultures.[4] Rachael Jack, a psychologist at the University of Glasgow, noted that Darwin's studies were based only on the expressions of Western Europeans, and assessed by Western European researchers. When she broadened the scope to include non-Western cultures, there were subtle but significant differences. Her conclusion was that each culture has its own fundamental expressions, but they are not necessarily shared by all cultures.[5]

Although it's true that some form of a smile is used in many cultures to express genuine happiness, studies also highlight the "social" smiles that most of us are conditioned to use to feign happiness from infancy. When and how often we use these social smiles throughout our lives has a lot to do with cultural programming. Differentiating between genuine expressions of happiness and feigned happiness is challenging, particularly if you are trying to translate a smile across cultures.

The next time you meet up with a friend, pay attention to why and how often you smile. Are you smiling because you are genuinely happy or just out of habit or obligation? Or are you using your smile to mask some other kind of emotion? Also take notice of your expectations of when your friend should smile, and what you think that smile means.

If you were raised in the United States, chances are you smile a lot. People in the United States are generally expected to greet everyone with a smile, whether making someone's acquaintance for the first time or reuniting with an old friend. Smiles are the gold standard in sales, marketing, and other kinds of business-related introductions (think of the widely touted slogan "customer service with a smile"). Whether genuine or perfunctory, smiles are requisite in many contexts and particularly expected of women in many cultures.

In places like Russia and Switzerland, however, greeting people with a smile is not always considered appropriate. Smiling without reason can be perceived as insincere. Despite the lack of a smile, a person from one of these cultures might be feeling perfectly happy and intending to be friendly. But you can imagine how someone programmed to expect to be greeted with a smile might interpret the blank expression as a sign of discontent and unfriendliness. During cross-cultural job interviews, smiling can result in major misinterpretations: a candidate who smiles repeatedly might be perceived in some cultures as having an affable personality and positive outlook, while in other cultures that same smiling candidate might be seen as insincere, untrustworthy, or just "off."

The use and meaning of smiles probably evolved differently across cultures for a wide variety of reasons. People in certain cultures are simply less emotionally expressive than others, so they are less likely to display a smile or any other revealing expression in public. And then there are those We-oriented cultures like Japan, where a large percentage of smiles are used to save face—to hide embarrassment, anger, or another negative emotion in social and business contexts. The social smile in these cultures can imply much more than just feigned happiness.

Our assumption that the intent and implications of a smile are the same across all cultures can get us into varying degrees of trouble, from minor misunderstandings to major issues. Around the globe, law enforcement and security officials are trained to read people's faces to uncover their true intentions and emotions. But if smiles and other expressions mean different things across cultures, officials need to apply a distinct deciphering procedure to accurately size up people they encounter from other cultures.

The upshot is, you can't always judge a person's intentions or happiness quotient by their smile, so remember to pause before you jump to any conclusions.

Don't Stand So Close to Me

Do you know someone who stands just a little too close to you during a conversation—so close that you can easily identify what they've had for lunch? Or maybe you know someone who always seems to stand noticeably farther away, even when you're having an intimate conversation.

Personal preferences play a role in the distance you maintain when you stand, sit, or walk with another person. Context plays a role too; your comfort level may change based on whether you interacting with a family member, friend, colleague, or someone from the opposite sex. But regardless of individual preferences and context, the foundation for our differing comfort levels around personal space are usually related to cultural programming.

People from "close" cultures are often comfortable conversing with someone at a mere elbow's length. If the distance is greater, they may unconsciously try to close the gap. At the opposite end of the spectrum, there are cultures in which people tend to maintain a larger buffer zone, sometimes as much as four feet or more from another person.

What happens when someone from a close-up culture gets together with someone from a far-apart culture? A very awkward dance ensues. I've watched Brazilians (a close-up culture) and Japanese (a far-apart culture) step on each other's toes and bump into walls as each tries to out-maneuver the other's spatial preferences.

Like so much of our cultural programming, we are barely aware of our spatial preferences until someone makes us feel uncomfortable by getting too close or too far away. To get a better idea of your own comfort zone, try this test:

Grab a friend or family member and stand facing each other. Stand far enough apart that you can extend your arm out until your finger-tips touch the person's shoulder. This arm's-length distance is usually preferred in places like the United States and Canada. How does that feel to you? Is this the right amount of space for a conversation at a party? How about between a salesperson and a customer? How about with a coworker or someone of the opposite sex?

Now, close the space so that you are an elbow's distance apart and see how it feels. Too close? Just right? This is the distance more typi-cal in places like Brazil and Greece.

Lastly, stand facing each other with enough distance between you so that you both can extend your arms out until your fingertips barely touch each other's. Too far? You are most likely to encounter this kind of distance in places like Japan and Korea—and in the Arab world when the two people are different genders.

Once you've identified your own spatial comfort zone, it's easier to recognize when another person is closing or widening the gap, sig-naling that you might need to override your own preferences to make them feel more at ease.

Touchy Subjects

I have many friends from Colombia who pull people toward them as they walk. They may link arms and place a hand on a shoulder or mid back, keeping their faces very close when they talk. It's the kind of touching and closeness that many people from the United

States expect only from people with whom they are more intimately involved. A lingering touch can have discomforting implications, especially if it's a man interacting with a woman. For women raised in Asian or Arab cultures, their discomfort would likely be even more pronounced.

But in many parts of Latin America, this kind of public touching is generally acceptable, regardless of gender and familiarity. Touching

DOUBLE MEANINGS

The following are some gestures that mean different things in different cultures.

- Slapping the palm of your hand on your closed fist (the flat part, by the thumb and first finger) is obscene in Azerbaijan and Brazil. In Cameroon it means "very much" or "a lot."

- Wagging an index finger means "be careful" or "attention" in Burkina Faso. In many parts of Latin America it simply means "no."

- Tapping the side of your head with your index finger: In France it usually means that someone is clever. In Italy it can imply that someone is crazy.

- For indicating a person's height, in Colombia people hold the palm vertically with the thumb on top (holding your palm face down is just for indicating the height of animals). In China and other places, the vertical open palm can suggest that you are pointing in a particular direction.

- Cupping your elbow is used to suggest someone is stingy in Mexico and many South American nations. In Austria and Germany, it is used to say someone's an idiot.

on the arm, shoulders, hands, and elbows is also very common during greetings, conversations and strolling; it is used to imply friendship at every level. This kind of touch is also acceptable in many African and Arab cultures, but it's often only between men. It's not uncommon to see men linking arms or holding hands with other men—something you rarely see in the United States, Canada, or Northern Europe, unless of course they are injured or inebriated and need physical support.

On the opposite end of the spectrum are the "keep your hands to yourself" cultures that prefer little or no touching, even when greeting and saying goodbye. During conversations touching is virtually nonexistent, and if it does occur, it can be a major faux pas. So unless you know the touching rules of a particular culture, keep your hands to yourself and let the other person make the first move!

To Look or Not to Look

My father, a Boston native, taught me to look people directly in the eyes when talking to them, especially adults. Halfway around the world in Japan, my friend Masahiro's father was telling him to do the opposite—to always look away when meeting people who were more senior.

To look or to look away: that is one of the most troublesome cross-cultural questions. In some cultures, direct eye contact is the way to go; it suggests confidence, respect, and interest in what the other person is saying. That same level of sustained eye contact is expected when talking to friends, colleagues, and others, regardless of age, stature, or gender. A lack of eye contact may suggest that a person is untrustworthy or lacks confidence or interest.

In other cultures, direct eye contact can be construed as a sign of disrespect or a threat, and it might be more appropriate to show respect by *avoiding* sustained eye contact. This may especially be called for when talking with someone older or more experienced than you, or of the opposite sex, unless you have an intimate or familial relationship with them. How we look someone in the eye depends on the situation, but people from the same culture tend to behave similarly in a surprising variety of contexts: from interviewing, to meetings, to casual exchanges with community members, to business transactions.

Over the years, I've heard from hundreds of sales professionals in the United States who are repeatedly irritated by the lack of eye contact from their buyers. Much of the time it breaks down along gender lines: male sellers feel frustrated that they can't get women to look them in the eye, and female sellers are offended that men won't make eye contact with them. While the buyers are merely trying to be respectful, the sellers don't read it that way. Meanwhile, the buyers may feel that the sellers are being disrespectful by trying so hard to catch their eye. Their mutual frustration sets a negative tone for the whole interaction.

The only way to prevent this kind of situation is to spend some time noting your own preferences and assumptions about what eye contact means in various scenarios. Once you know what they are, you'll be better able to catch yourself in auto-pilot mode and to adjust as needed during cross-cultural interactions.

Greet and Be Greeted

The proper ways to greet and say goodbye to people from different cultures can be easily looked up in a guidebook. Heading to India? You might want to take the time to learn the *pranamasana*, a gesture used to say hello and goodbye. To offer it, press your hands together with the palms touching, fingers pointing upward and thumbs close to your chest. In Kuwait, the United Arab Emirates, and New Zealand people sometimes rub noses as a greeting. Then there's the kissing and hugging: Mexicans plant a kiss on one cheek, many French go for two air kisses on alternating cheeks, while in the Netherlands it's three. In the ancient capital city of Nara, Japan, even the wild deer have been culturally programmed to bow when greeting their human compatriots and tourists (and as a way of saying thanks for the food).

The most commonly used greeting worldwide, however, is the handshake, and it's the one of the safest to use if you don't know someone's background—but only if the person is the same gender as you, because touching between genders is taboo in many cultures if the parties are not related. When greeting across genders, a slight dip of the head or a bow is a better idea.

Once you go in for a handshake, there are still nuances to consider, as noted in chapter one. Different ways of shaking hands can have different implications depending on the culture. These variations can have a big impact on our impression of someone, especially when we are meeting them for the first time. For me, the grip has to be just the right level of firmness: too light, and it suggests a slipperiness of character or passiveness; too strong, and I am more prone to label that person as aggressive. The rub is that what *you* might perceive as either a weak or an overly strong handshake may simply be the norm in certain cultures and hold no notable significance.

Besides firmness, the length of a handshake can also have implications. If you offer a shake that's too quick (less than one pump), in some cultures it may suggest that you are not interested in pursuing the relationship. Conversely, a handshake that lingers—sometimes even turning into a handhold—can suggest genuine interest in building a business or platonic relationship. But that same lingering handshake can trigger discomfort in other cultures, prompting the receiver to question the motives of the person holding on.

Next time you shake someone's hand, notice your grip and also notice what the other person does. Does it feel just right to you? Like everything else, after you recognize your own preferences, you can open your mind to other ways of handshaking, which will make you less likely to judge someone's character based on your own cultural bias.

One technique that I find useful when it comes to getting the handshake just right is mirroring. If someone extends their hand, start with a neutral grip and match the person's grasp, firming up or relaxing as needed. If they pull away quickly or linger, I simply do the same. If someone offers a bow or slight head nod instead of a handshake, I do as they do.

Mirroring is an essential tool that can be used not only when it comes to greeting people, but with all sorts of nonverbal communication. If someone doesn't look you in the eyes, consider averting your own gaze. If someone is standing at a distance that you deem too far apart, don't automatically close the gap—and vice versa. Notice what gestures they are using or not using and follow suit. You get the idea. It's all about following the other person's lead—a technique you can even apply to things like time orientation, as you'll see in the next chapter. That's not to say that you should mirror every behavior you observe, but when you do mirror, you'll need to do so discreetly so it doesn't seem like you are merely imitating someone. Mirroring requires some additional attentiveness, but it's a minimal investment that can help you get off on the right foot and go a long way toward building strong connections across cultures.

CULTURE KEYS

Quick Tips for Communicating Without Words

Eye Contact   If someone doesn't look you in the eyes, consider averting your gaze too.

Beckoning   Avoid all nonverbal beckoning unless you are totally sure how it will be interpreted.

Pointing   Your safest bet is to point using an open hand.

Yes or No   Don't rely on head movements; it's better to verbally confirm if someone is saying yes or no.

Counting   When possible, confirm numbers verbally or in writing.

Smiling   You can't always judge a person's intentions or happiness quotient by their smile, so pause and consider alternate implications before jumping to conclusions.

Touching   Unless you know the touching etiquette of a particular culture, keep your hands to yourself and let others make the first move.

Personal space   If someone is standing at a distance, don't automatically close the gap. If you feel someone is too close, know that it's not always cause for alarm, and if you feel the need to back away, then do it gradually.

Greetings   Use the mirroring strategy: If someone extends their hand, shake it with a neutral grip and firm up or relax your grip to match theirs. If someone bows or dips their head, do as they do. This is the safest greeting between unrelated men and women.

FIVE

Now or Later

How perceptions of time can warp across cultures

The island nation of Madagascar that lies off of Africa's eastern shore is well known among biologists for its incredible diversity of animal and plant species. But for cultural psychologists, Madagascar is perhaps better known for its empty fuel pumps.

Øyvind Dahl is a Norwegian psychologist who observed stark differences in the way that people in rural Madagascar tend to view time, in contrast to most Western cultures.[1] While conducting research there in the early 1990s, Dahl noticed that many of the fuel stations outside of the city were perpetually out of gas.[2] A hose slung over the top of the pump was a telltale sign that there was no fuel to be had. Most of us probably would have chalked it up to a scarcity of petroleum in this developing nation, but Dahl's curiosity was piqued, and he decided to ask the manager about it. His conversation went like this:

DAHL: Why isn't there more gas?

GAS STATION MANAGER: Because it is empty. Look, nothing left.

DAHL: But haven't you ordered new provisions?

GAS STATION MANAGER: Of course. I did that two weeks ago. But they are always slow to react in Antananarivo [the capital].

DAHL: So why did you not order the gas a couple of weeks before?

GAS STATION MANAGER: Well, it was not empty then!

DAHL: Why don't you order new provisions when you know that you are approaching empty? So that there will be no interruptions?

GAS STATION MANAGER: Sometimes very few people come to buy gas, and sometimes many people come. So you never know when it's empty. But when it's empty, it's empty, and you have to order more gas. In the meantime, I will hang up the hose so that people know. It will come—some day. Time will show.[3]

Dahl had similar conversations with other gas station managers. He also found that local shopkeepers did the same thing: they would wait until provisions like medicine and farm equipment had completely run out before ordering a new supply.[4] Dahl's assessment of this tendency to wait for a triggering event (like running out of fuel or medicine) before taking action was a direct reflection of the people's perception of time. In these communities, Dahl theorized that time is considered to be cyclical, like the seasons—an ever-repeating loop marked by events that signal people to take action, like the way changes in weather signal the best time to plant seeds or harvest fruit. In contrast to Dahl's European view of time in which time is always moving forward away from the past and toward the future, he theorized that people from Madagascar have a more cyclical view of time that blurs the delineations between past, present, and future. In this view, time itself lets people know when they need to take action to meet the needs of changing circumstances.

Confused yet? Don't worry. The main point is there are many different ways of thinking about and expressing time, something most of us do on autopilot as a result of our cultural programming. Dahl notes that the Malagasy view of time doesn't necessarily apply to all aspects of life in rural regions, but it occurs frequently enough to be dubbed "Malagasy time" or *fotoana gasy* as locals refer to it.[5] (The people of Madagascar are called the Malagasy, as the country was formerly the Malagasy Republic.) Dahl's line of questioning with the gas station manager underscores how someone who sees time as linear would be hard put to comprehend the behaviors associated with nonlinear perceptions of time—thereby priming the proverbial pump for frustration.

Differing perceptions of time—and the way it impacts our behaviors—can lead to an array of culture crashes. The most obvious and frequently encountered problems relate to punctuality. My parents found themselves in the midst of a punctuality crash when they first moved our family from Boston, Massachusetts, to Bogotá, Colombia, in the 1980s. Not long after arriving, my parents were invited to a dinner party to welcome them to the community. When my father asked what time the party was called for, the Colombians responded, "*Por ahi a las 8:00*" (around 8:00 P.M.). My parents showed up at their house bearing wine at 8:00 on the dot, just as they would have for a party in the United States. The hostess answered the door wearing a bathrobe, having just emerged from a shower and clearly not prepared for guests.

My parents waited patiently in the living room for the next hour, feeling slightly embarrassed and a little annoyed, and getting hungrier by the minute. Other guests eventually started to arrive just as their blood sugar levels had begun to bottom out. Thankfully, appetizers were served soon after that, although dinner didn't come until around 11:00 P.M., followed by coffee and dessert well past midnight.

This was my parents' first introduction to "Colombia time." A perceived looseness about watching the clock is a phenomenon that many people from the United States experience when they interact with people from Latin American countries. It can be a constant source of frustration for people who misinterpret the act of showing up too late (or too early) as disrespectful, without knowing that it simply stems from varying perceptions of time. Invited to many subsequent parties during the twelve years that they lived in Bogotá, my parents learned that these kinds of social gatherings almost never started on time, and that arriving more than an hour "late" was not only acceptable and respectable, but expected. As a survival strategy, my parents adjusted their notion of "on time," and always made sure to snack and nap before heading out.

Although you may have never heard the expressions "Colombia time" or "Malagasy time," you are probably familiar with expressions like "a New York minute" or "island time." These expressions speak to the distinct ways that different cultures perceive time, and they are often used to let foreigners know that they need to adjust their clocks accordingly when they are in that country. When people relocate or immigrate to other countries, they bring with them their deeply embedded views of time. Eventually they may be able to override their instincts and modify their behaviors as my parents did, but the roots of their earliest programming will remain, and they will probably continue to create minor culture crashes. The perception of time is one of the toughest cultural habits to shake.

We all integrate our perceptions of time into our lives in different ways, related partly to culture and partly to personal predilections. Consider your expectations around punctuality, for example. When do you arrive at parties, business meetings, or other functions? On the dot? Five minutes early? One hour late? How late is too late, and how early is too early? Some of us pride ourselves on getting things done way in advance, while others wait until the last minute, or even later. You might be someone who tries to accomplish many tasks at once, or someone who prefers to do things one at a time. And what about how your sense of the past, present, and future impacts your outlook on life? Some people continually look toward the past as a guide to how to proceed in their daily lives. Others are more oriented to the present, harboring a sense of immediacy that pervades all of their actions and responses. And then there are those who generally keep their outlook fixed on the future, placing more emphasis on the long-term outcomes of decisions and actions.

Madagascar and Colombia are not the only places where people view time as more fluid—something that doesn't always need to be micromanaged by the clock or calendar. There are cultures in every part of the world that share this perception of time to varying degrees and with a diverse array of nuances. To keep things simple, I refer to cultures that tend to see time as relatively abundant, malleable, and/or cyclical as *Later* cultures. In these cultures, the way that people tend to live their lives is shaped by the notion that there is always more time later.

For most people raised in the United States, however, the notion of time moving in an endless loop is pretty hard to wrap their brains around. That's because in the United States, time tends to be viewed as relatively limited and linear. Time moves on a continuum: the past flowing out behind them and the future stretching before them. And while time may march on endlessly, the chunk of time people are personally allotted each day—or in their lifetimes—does not. Time is a commodity that can be spent, saved, wasted, or used wisely. Time is something precious that must be used carefully and efficiently. As a result, it's generally expected that deadlines, plans, and schedules will be adhered to. Once time is in the past, it is irretrievable. There is an imperative to get things done now, before the time disappears. For simplicity's sake I refer to cultures where people tend to perceive time in this way as *Now* cultures, enabling us to more easily understand and explore these perceptions.

Time as a Prized Commodity

I recently took a flight from San Francisco to Denver to attend a conference. The plane was delayed taking off, and I became anxious that I was going to miss the opening presentation. As the minutes ticked by, I could see other passengers becoming restless too, looking at their watches and shaking their heads. About twenty minutes later we were cleared for takeoff. About an hour later the pilot turned on the speaker to make an announcement: "Good news, everyone: the tail wind is strong, and it looks like we will be able to make up the lost time."

Sound familiar? If so, you know what came next: smiles, some applause, and a collective sigh of relief from the passengers. Now think about what the pilot said. He implied that time is something that can be "made up." Have you ever questioned this premise or considered that not everybody thinks of time as something that can be lost or made up like money invested in the stock market?

Expressions like this one underscore the degree to which perceptions of time become engrained not only in the fabric of a culture, but also in our brains. No matter how I try, I cannot override my emotional response—my sheer glee—at the idea of making up time. I'm always looking for ways to find more time in my day to finish all my tasks. It's one reason hundreds of thousands of people in the United States have bought the book *The 4-Hour Workweek*.[6] People (myself included) are chasing the elusive dream of finding more hours in the day. We let time control our actions, adapting and adjusting to the demands of schedules and deadlines.

Here are a few other expressions commonly used in places like the United States, Canada, and parts of Europe that underscore this kind of thinking:

Time is money.

Time and tide wait for no man.

The time is now.

We need to save time.

Don't waste time.

Time is running out.

These expressions make little or no sense to cultures on the other end of the spectrum, where time is perceived as being cyclical and/or less limited. In Later cultures, time is more of a flexible entity than a fixed commodity. When time is considered ongoing and easily adjustable, there's less fear of its running out—and adherence to schedules becomes less important. Even schedules that I think of as set in stone, like public transportation schedules, can be a moving target in some Later cultures. When I was living in the Caribbean during my teenage years, I often visited the island of Jamaica, where people generally seemed less beholden to schedules—especially outside of the capital. It was only after several visits to Jamaica that I stopped asking when the bus was going to appear at the bus stop, knowing that the answer was always "Soon come," along with a look that implied that I should relax.

Mexico is another place where schedules tend to be less rigid in daily life, a sentiment underscored by the expression "*Darle tiempo al tiempo*." It literally translates as "give time to time," but what it really means is that there's no need to rush. Let time run its natural course, and things will sort themselves out as they should. Hurrying doesn't help.

Here are some other sayings from other cultures that underscore views of time that tend toward the Later end of the spectrum.

When God made time, he made plenty of it. (China)

What flares up fast extinguishes soon. (Turkey)

A ripe melon falls by itself. (Zimbabwe)

Man has responsibility, not power, over time. (Native American)

Depending on our personal programming around time, we may be critical of how others manage and perceive it. But others will be equally critical of your views of time. Your best bet for rising above the fray of judgments and misinterpretations is to start by getting better acquainted with your inner time zone.

Know Your Time Zone

Living in a Now culture is an unfortunate fate for someone like my wife, who is perpetually and apologetically running late. Although she has a strong sense of time as a limited commodity, her personal time management habits poke through each time she finds herself in a rush to get somewhere. She becomes anxious every time she runs more than ten minutes late, because she knows that she is not meeting the cultural expectation, and she is being disrespectful of others' time. On one occasion, her friend—a very punctual person—felt so disrespected by my wife's showing up late for the umpteenth time that her friend didn't speak to her for a week. The bottom line is that although my wife's personal clock runs on its own schedule, she is still beholden to and impacted by general expectations about time in her culture.

The funny thing is that even when my wife considers herself on time, she is actually running late according to the clock (usually by four or five minutes). And there are plenty of other Americans who, like my wife, perceive a certain amount of time as a standard grace period. It's puzzling to those of us whose personal clocks are geared for precise punctuality—that is, until you consider the phenomenon of "segmentation."

Over the years, social scientists like Edward Hall and Robert Levine have theorized that people segment their time in different ways, which in turn results in differing perceptions of being early and late.[7] In his book *The Silent Language*, Hall observed that Americans divide time as follows: "there are eight time sets in regards to punctuality and length of appointments: on time, five, ten, fifteen, twenty, thirty, forty-five minutes, and one hour early or late."[8]

Essentially, what he's saying is that people in the United States mentally partition time into these increments, so that if you are late by five minutes, you are late by only one time segment; if you are late by ten minutes, you are late by two segments; fifteen minutes late is three segments late; and so on. So, when my wife shows up four minutes late, in her mind she's not technically late by even one segment yet. I, however, consider half a segment as being late, which has been known to cause some minor culture crashes in our household.

While there are plenty of noticeable differences among people of the same cultures when it comes to perceptions of time, Hall was primarily focused on how these differences break down along cultural lines. In his book, he recounts the story of an American ambassador in an unnamed country who was infuriated because local diplomats would always show up an hour late to meetings.[9] Here is Hall's assessment of the perception of time in this culture:

An hour's tardiness in their system is equivalent to five minutes by ours, fifty to fifty-five minutes to four minutes, forty-five minutes to three minutes, and so on for daytime official visits. By their standards the local diplomats felt they couldn't arrive exactly on time; this punctuality might be interpreted locally as an act relinquishing their freedom of action to the United States. But they didn't want to be insulting—an hour late would be too late—so they arrived fifty minutes late. As a consequence the ambassador said, "How can you depend on these people when they arrive an hour late for an appointment and then just mutter something? They don't even give you a full sentence of apology!" He couldn't help feeling this way, because in American time, fifty to fifty-five minutes late is the insult period, at the extreme end of the duration scale; yet in the country we are speaking of it's just right.

Hall never identifies this unknown country at the other end of the spectrum from the United States (I could venture some guesses). Hall did, however, theorize that people from Arab cultures in the Mediterranean such as Morocco, Tunisia, and Libya use scales of time that don't differentiate between a long time and a very long time,[10] in stark contrast to the five- to ten-minute increments of lateness that people from the United States use as their barometer. Social psychologist Robert Levine made a similar assertion about U.S. and Arab cultures, but he added that people from Arab cultures break time down into fifteen-minute increments when assessing their own punctuality.[11]

Their combined conclusions have long been widely accepted, but some social scientists wondered if those findings would still hold up today based on more current data. In 2012, three university professors from around the world conducted a study with three hundred students from Morocco, the United States, and Estonia and found that "the Moroccans in the study were more likely than Americans to mentally partition an hour into 15-minute segments."[12]

In other words, an American who arrives ten minutes after the appointed time is late by what they called "two units of psychological time." But a Moroccan who is running late by two perceived units of time would arrive thirty minutes late. The Estonians seemed to fall somewhere in between the other two cultures. Although the study was limited, it does generally uphold the assertions made decades ago by Hall and Levine.

All of these studies underscore the notion that people from different cultures abide by different clocks and measures of lateness. Bearing this in mind may help you curtail your frustration when someone shows up early or late by your standards. The broader takeaway is that we are all conditioned to perceive time in ways we are barely aware of, and it's only by sizing up our personal clocks that we can adjust our expectations and behaviors in order to avoid a crash.

While we may have a vague idea of whether we tend toward the Now or Later end of the spectrum, it's usually only in relation to other people from our home culture. When *crossing* cultures, those differences can be much more drastic. Try answering the following questions to get a clearer idea of your Now-Later orientation and a sense of where you fall on what I call the "time warp" scale. Although tendencies may shift, depending on the situation, these questions are still a good starting point.

1. You are in a business meeting with another person. Your phone rings with a call from an old friend. You:

   a. Answer it and talk with the person calling.

    b. Answer it and immediately tell the person you will call them back.

    c. Ignore it and let it go to voicemail.

2. You are waiting for a bus and there is no schedule posted. You:

    a. Ask others at the stop if they know when the bus will come, and constantly check your watch. You feel frustrated.

    b. Wait ten minutes and then decide to walk or look for a taxi.

    c. Turn on some music and relax until the bus comes.

3. You've missed your bus or train by a few seconds. You're not in a rush to be somewhere. Your thoughts are:

    a. *Oh sh*t. That really sucks.*

    b. *That's too bad.*

    c. *No worries. There's always another one.*

4. You recognize that you will not be able to meet a deadline that has been set. You:

    a. Immediately let everyone involved know and share contingency plans.

    b. Share the news with everyone involved just moments before the deadline.

    c. Let people know only after you've missed the deadline—and only if or when they ask for the deliverable.

5. You are waiting for a colleague to join you in a scheduled meeting, and they are late. You:

    a. Text or call them two to five minutes after the appointed time, and leave if there is no response.

    b. Text or call them ten to fifteen minutes after the appointed time; if there is no response, leave.

c. Wait fifteen to thirty minutes (without calling or texting) before leaving.

Now review your answers. Give yourself zero points for every "a" answer, one point for every "b" answer, and two points for every "c."

Have a look at where your total falls in the following scale:

0   1   2   3   4   5   6   7   8   9   10

Now   **Later**
Time is more limited/less flexible   Time is less limited/more flexible

While our personal clocks all run differently, the behavior of people from different cultures does consistently fall on the spectrum in certain ways that are continuously reinforced at work and in daily life.

As an example, let's say you have a meeting at 9:00 A.M. and you leave your home in time to get to work, but the train or the bus is running late. You burst into the meeting room, blaming your tardiness on the bus. Your boss shoots you the "liar look"—she probably assumes that you just overslept or opted for an all-too-leisurely pancake breakfast. If you live in Japan, Germany, or parts of Switzerland and France, however, and your train is running late, when you board it you may be handed a "late card" or "certificate of delay." You would then hand this to your boss—and there would be no doubt about why you missed the first half the meeting. It's interesting to note that a delay of one to five minutes will most often get you the certificate of delay in Japan, where the average train delay on some major lines is a mere thirty-six seconds,[13] while in France the delay has to be at least fifteen minutes before you are offered any proof.[14] In Switzerland, trains are expected to arrive on time as much as possible, and if delayed, then no more than three minutes behind schedule.[15]

The Swiss, who have come to dominate the high-end watch-making industry, take "being on time" very seriously, leaning heavily toward the Now end of the spectrum. In Swiss French, punctuality is reinforced through language; you are either *avant l'heure* (before the hour) or *après l'heure* (after the hour)—expressions used to indicate that either you are on time or you're not, implying that there is little allowance for missed minutes.

That's not to say that the Swiss never find themselves running late, but chances are they would feel more stressed out by being in this position than someone from a culture that didn't place such a high value on being punctual. At the other end of the spectrum are places like Jamaica where common phrases like "soon come" reflect a relatively looser attitude toward time.

The reasons *why* certain cultures experience time the way they do are interesting to consider. What values and other reasons underlie differing perceptions of time? The answers can be complex and varied, but it's worth examining the inner workings of some of these cultural clocks, if only to get you thinking more deeply about your own cultural wiring.

Whether a culture falls more toward the Now or the Later end of the spectrum often has to do with whether people place more value on accomplishing a specific task or cultivating relationships, just as Me-We tendencies do (although not all We cultures are also Later oriented—Japan is a prime example of a We culture oriented toward punctuality). In Later cultures, if a need or opportunity arises to build or nurture a relationship, it tends to take precedence in daily life over punctuality or getting something done quickly. This doesn't mean that people in Now cultures don't care about relationships; it just means that they are less likely to spend time tending a relationship until the more urgent task at hand has been accomplished—or if spending time on that relationship has the potential to screw up a schedule.

Other drivers of Now and Later orientation may have to do with the evolution of regional history and politics, like a desire to create a sense of order amidst chaos caused by perpetual warfare.[16] There are also theories that point to the tendency for cultures with high levels of economic development to be more Now oriented (time = money), while in less economically developed or less stable nations the value of time may lie more in people's ability to "spend" it building relationships. In *A Geography of Time*, Robert Levine points out that in places where employment opportunities are scarcer and less reliable, jobs don't improve well-being as reliably as family and friends do. He found that places with vibrant economies tend to value time more, and vice versa; and that the wealthier the society, the faster things tend to move.[17]

Other factors may also shape the way different cultures perceive and organize time, such as population density, climate, and religious beliefs. Friends of mine who live and work in Mexico City tell me that one reason everyone is always running late there is that the traffic is so bad that you can never be sure whether it will take ten minutes or two hours to get somewhere.

If we can keep in mind that there are differing values and other factors that underlie our expectations and perceptions of time across cultures—including our own—we are less likely to make snap judgments about someone's behavior that can cause us to lash out in anger or label people as inefficient, inconsiderate, or over-eager, depending on our point of view. This may also offer some enlightenment for people like me who experience time anxiety in our own cultures because our personal views of time are sometimes at odds with cultural norms.

Taking Your Time at Work

No matter where I am in the world or with whom I am working, when I am preparing to run a workshop I always ask whether I can expect people in the company to be punctual, and if not, how long I should wait before starting. The answer varies widely from company to company and even within departments of the same company. I've heard expressions like the "software seven" (minutes) and the "engineering eight" at different companies in the United States. In some companies I'm told to start right on the hour, and in others to hold fire for fifteen.

There are many reasons why companies within the same culture may have different takes on time. Sometimes it's because people need extra time to physically get from one meeting to another. Other times it may be based on the personal clock of the head of the organization or department. No matter the reason, every organization has its own expectations for promptness as well as other time-related activities, including when the workday starts and ends, how much time someone takes for lunch, length of vacations, and so on. When you start working for any company you have to learn the nuances of how they view time, but when you work for a company based in or staffed by people from other cultures things can be even more challenging.

Workday lunch breaks are often a big point of contention between people from Now and Later cultures. I've worked with people from the United States who fume over what they perceive as excessively long lunch breaks taken by their Brazilian colleagues (usually one-and-a-half to two hours). People from the United States tend to think of lunch breaks of an hour or more as indulgent or reserved only for special occasions. This perception leads them to accuse their Brazilian counterparts of being inefficient and lacking dedication to the job. In the United States, when people eat lunch at their desks it's generally seen as a sign of dedication—that they have prioritized work over all of their personal necessities and pleasures.

On the flip side, I've worked with Brazilians who complain about how their counterparts from the United States eat at their desks and refuse invitations to join them for lunch. The Brazilians interpret their colleagues' behavior as a lack of dedication to the team—or a lack of interest in building strong relationships, which would yield better results at work.

As with every other culture crossing, the key to avoiding this kind of crash is to hit the pause button before making judgments about how people use their time, and consider the message you may be inadvertently sending out via your own behavior. If you get the vibe that you are working with people from a Now culture, try your best to be on time for meetings, return emails and calls promptly, and be quick about your break times. If you are dealing with a company or a boss from a Later culture, they may have more tolerance (and so should you) for late arrivals to meetings, delayed responses to communications, and lengthy lunch breaks, which are generally better for digestion than scarfing down some food at your desk anyway.

Fast Buy or Slow Sell?

If you sell things for a living in the United States, creating a sense of urgency is one of the most effective tools in your kit. Admonitions like "this house will probably go very quickly" or "demand is high and the inventory is low, so I would act now if I were you" have long been a failsafe method to nudge potential buyers into a purchase. When I was searching for a home, just a subtle suggestion of urgency was sometimes enough to set my nerves aflutter, even if I didn't even like the house very much. But real estate agents and other kinds of salespeople in the United States who have always depended on this tactic are now finding that it no longer works as reliably, because they aren't selling to the same pool of potential buyers. Today, a large percentage of buyers are recent immigrants. Documented immigrants comprise about 14 percent of the U.S. population and growing[18] (by 2050, roughly one of every five U.S. residents will be foreign born[19]).

Many of these immigrants hail from Later-oriented cultures—places where they are much less likely to be swayed by time pressures.

Next time you are considering a purchase, think about how you are affected by a sense of urgency, whether real or fabricated. People from Now cultures easily fall prey to scarcity ploys and marketing strategies like "this offer is only good for the next thirty minutes and open to the first five callers!" Or how about the "last one in stock" line, or the perpetual (and often questionable) "going out of business" sale?

Even though you know that the same exact offer may still stand a few weeks later, this marketing technique plays right into the fear that time is rapidly running out, and you must act now.

In the United States, this fear is also connected to the desire for immediate gratification. Despite the adage "Good things come to those who wait," most people in the United States prefer *not* to wait. It's this mindset that spawned innovations such as drive-through restaurants and banking, which began in the United States in the 1930s.[20] These days there are even drive-through wedding chapels in Las Vegas for those who truly can't wait to tie the knot. 7-Eleven, a convenience store chain ubiquitous throughout the United States and now in many other parts of the world, was one of the first stores to have extended hours from 7 A.M. to 11 P.M.[21] Today, 7-Eleven and other convenience stores are often open even later, further accommodating the late-night whims of Now-oriented people living in urban centers around the globe. At the extreme end of the Now spectrum are places like New York City, where most residents will tell you that they find it comforting to know they can get a slice of pizza and a roll of double-ply toilet paper *any* time they need or want it. No matter if the pizza tastes like cardboard or the roll of toilet paper costs $5.00—people are often happy just knowing it's available right now.

In recent years I've heard from countless sales and marketing people frustrated by the fact that their Now tactics aren't effective when selling to people in immigrant communities. These potential buyers are likely from Later cultures in which rushing things can backfire, especially when it comes to making a significant purchase. The right time to buy or sell is often more influenced by factors like auspicious dates, favorable numbers, and getting advice or buy-in from others. People from Later-oriented cultures may be wary of transactions that move too quickly or of people who pressure them with questionable time constraints.

That said, it is possible to facilitate the purchase in other ways with customers who are less compelled by urgency. The key is to discover what is important to the buyer rather than simply relying on the scarcity ploy. Look and listen for cues like whether the buyer asks you personal questions, which may imply that they want to get to know you a bit better and develop a sense of trust. Notice if the customers spend time discussing the benefits of certain dates and numbers, and consider how you can adjust the offer to accommodate those concerns. If they mention needing to talk to others, schedule a time in the near future when others can see the product too and join in the conversation. Ask questions to try to get at what's most important to the customer—you might be surprised by what you discover.

The bottom line is, you'll have a better chance of influencing someone to make a purchase—or do anything else—if you look for cultural cues like those we've discussed (as opposed to projecting your own culture onto them) and adjust your tactics accordingly. The more you work or interact with people from a particular culture, the more attuned you will become to these cues if your mind is primed to spot them. Of course, when it comes to influencing people, this strategy is useful not only as it relates to perceptions of time, but also for all of the ways that culture defines how we do business and navigate interactions in other aspects of our daily lives.

CULTURE KEY

Quick Tips for Navigating Time Across Cultures

Nows working with Laters	Laters working with Nows
Understand that schedules and deadlines are less of a priority and expect changes or missed deadlines.	Adhering to schedules and deadlines may be considered extremely important, so try to avoid changes or missed deadlines.
If deadlines are truly not adjustable, communicate the impact and consequences of the delay, highlighting how it may impact the relationship if a deadline is missed.	If deadlines won't be met, communicate this as soon as possible to minimize damage to relationships or the sense of trust. Failure to acknowledge a missed deadline could be detrimental.
Be prepared to wait longer than you normally would for others to arrive at meetings and social events—and for responses to emails and other kinds of messages that you send.	Arriving just a few minutes late to meetings or certain social events can be construed as disrespectful. If possible, let them know if you're delayed. If you receive an email or message that you're not able to respond to right away, send a note to acknowledge it was received.
Be open to the idea that multiple tasks can be under way simultaneously and achieved in a less linear way.	Consider completing one task before starting a new one (when possible), emphasizing a sense of order.

Nows working with Laters	Laters working with Nows
When trying to influence Laters, the notion of urgency may be ineffectual. Instead, identify and facilitate other needs that are important, such as building consensus and relationships.	When trying to influence Nows, it's useful to convey a sense of urgency, playing on their view of time as fleeting.

SIX

Respect, Rank, and Ritual

The implications of formality at work and in everyday life

I have a British colleague who loves to reminisce about his first week of work at a Silicon Valley computer maker in the 1980s. The office was staffed by employees who either hailed from California or had been living there long enough to have embraced the state's relaxed style. You can imagine the staff's raised eyebrows and stifled chuckles when my friend walked in dressed in a three-piece suit. To them, he looked as if he was heading to a black tie affair or a James Bond look-alike contest.

Throughout the day his colleagues joked about his attire, assuming he would get the message that he could wear more casual clothes. He recalls many of the staff being dressed in jeans and flip-flops. The next day he lost the vest but kept the suit and tie. More encouragement by his coworkers led him to ditch the jacket and swap it for a sweater. When he was pressed further to relax his style, he finally hit his limit and shot back, "Just so you know, for me, this is informal!"

Our programming around formality plays a role in so many aspects of our lives, affecting not just the way we dress, but also how we greet and interact with others, serve and eat food, give and receive gifts, and simply walk down the street. Many of our expectations and habits concerning formality are connected to our deep-rooted cultural programming. As a result, slight miscommunications and even more significant culture crashes can easily occur when people from different ends of the formality spectrum cross paths.

Before we dive into the details of how these differences play out across cultures, it's helpful to understand what formality and informality mean to you—and how to identify them. The word *formality* is generally used to describe an observance of established customs, conventions, or rules of etiquette. That, in my opinion, is a very formal definition. So let's get down to what it really means in the context of our day-to-day lives.

Most of us can identify formal or informal behavior when we see it in the context of our own culture. It's particularly easy to spot formal behaviors in contrast to more informal behaviors. We often refer to the set of formal behaviors that we use in various contexts as "etiquette." If you display proper etiquette, it means you are behaving, dressing, or speaking in a way that is considered to be polite in a particular setting. But what constitutes formal behavior or proper etiquette in one culture may actually be considered relatively informal in another, or vice versa. The example of my British friend's experience in that Silicon Valley start-up is a simple illustration of that.

Think about other behaviors that you might be quick to label as "formal" or "proper," and how often you use or expect to see these behaviors. For me, easily identifiable formal behaviors include use of titles like Mr. or Ms., holding oneself upright as opposed to a slouching or lounging posture, speaking in hushed tones as opposed to being loud and boisterous, eating with utensils versus hands, and repeated use of polite language such as "thank you" and "please" to express consideration of others. For someone from another culture, their telltale signs of proper etiquette may include actions such as bowing deeply, standing rather than sitting, avoiding direct eye contact, and removing shoes in certain places. While there are general similarities between certain expressions of formality across cultures (such as the use of honorifics, offering guests a place of honor), the nuances and frequency of use can be extremely variable. In some cultures, behaviors perceived as formal are reserved for certain situations and ceremonial events, while in other cultures behaviors like these may be in play on a daily basis.

Navigating cultural differences related to the use of formal or informal behaviors can be challenging, but the bigger, underlying obstacles are the different ways that we communicate and perceive hidden messages through those behaviors. One of the most common messages conveyed by formal behavior is *respect*, including respect for places, traditions, or people. When it comes to human interactions, people may be authentically moved to use formal behaviors and other protocol to show deference for others, but it's frequently done out of a sense of obligation—a social imperative to show respect for someone's higher rank or status related to things like experience, job titles, and age. These formal protocols are often a means of acknowledging that one person has more influencing power than another. Using formality as an expression of respect for rank is an essential survival skill in cultures in which a social hierarchy defines the way people interact with each other.

In these cultures, varying degrees of deference may be required based on the extent to which people expect and accept that there is an unequal distribution of power. This phenomenon is known to sociologists as *power distance*—a term coined by Geert Hofstede as part of his IBM study[1]—and this factor also plays a role in the other topics discussed in this book.

In other cultures, however, formality may be downplayed as a way of purposefully disassociating from anything that smacks of social hierarchy. Although formality may be used to show respect in certain limited circumstances, the lack of formality is used to flatten any sense of social hierarchy. I think one of the main reasons U.S. culture is relatively informal is because the country's British "founders" wanted to escape the confines of a strict class system. As the culture evolved, *in*formality has been increasingly used as a tool for asserting the ideal of equality over hierarchy.

As an example, in many U.S. workplaces it may be totally acceptable to refer to your boss by their first name and even gently tease them. This informal behavior may even be welcomed by the boss, who doesn't want to come off as "above" everyone else. In other cultures, however, the informal and rank-breaking nature of this behavior would be considered totally disrespectful, no matter how long you had been working with your boss. Without knowledge of the underlying meanings associated with informality in the United States, a boss from a more formal culture might interpret the lack of formal etiquette as extremely rude and unacceptable. Conversely, someone from the United States might perceive a colleague who is more deferential toward their boss as being excessively and artificially polite.

The bottom line is that we are all conditioned to perceive formality as a positive or negative depending on our culture and the context. I found a good illustration of the negative association common in the United States when I looked up the word "formality" in the Oxford English/American online dictionary. Here are the first two definitions that come up:

1. The *rigid* observance of rules of *convention* or etiquette; and
1.1 *Stiffness* of behavior or style.

Notice the words "rigid" and "stiff"? In U.S. culture, the words "rigid" and "stiff"—and even the implication of being "conventional"—can have a decidedly negative connotation. In other cultures, words like "proper," "appropriate," and "official" might be more likely to appear in a definition—these words may have a more positive connotation in that culture.

People from different cultures tend to interpret formality in a positive or negative way for a wide variety of reasons, many having to do with context. For example, think about how you use varying levels of formality to greet someone, depending on your level of intimacy with that person. How would you greet a new acquaintance as opposed to an old friend? If you are like me, you modify what you say, your gestures, and even your facial expression to something you deem more formal when meeting someone new. This formality also implies a form of respect, but that's not to say you don't respect your old friend. You may have great respect for your friend; it's just that you no longer need to use formal cues to acknowledge it. Of course, that's just how it works in *my* culture. It would not be safe to assume that I have carte blanche to be *in*formal with old friends from other cultures, or that the way I express formality or informality will be perceived in a way that matches my intent.

Formality pitfalls are many and sundry, but you have a fighting chance of navigating these potential crashes if you take the time to figure out what formality means to you.

Figuring Out Your Formality Zone

The first question to answer is, do you generally think of formality as a positive or negative? Although it often depends on the situation, in our day-to-day lives most of us have some kind of gut reaction to behaviors or appearances that we construe as formal or informal. Let's use dress as an example again. If you think someone's clothes are formal, how does that inform your perception of them? If they tend to dress formally for a community gathering at a park, does it suggest to you that they are uptight or just very refined in their style? If someone dresses informally in a work environment, does it suggest to you that they don't take the job seriously, or that they are trying to appear humble and relaxed?

Consider how you dress in various contexts and the message you *think* you send through your choices. Would you wear the same thing for an interview that you would wear to dinner with friends? Would you wear the same thing to a class at school as you would to a baseball game or soccer match? Do you feel sufficiently formal if you wear jeans to work? Why or why not? What does wearing jeans "say" in this particular setting?

Dress codes can vary widely from culture to culture. For example, unless you lived in Cuba, you wouldn't know that wearing an untucked, typically short-sleeved, patterned guayabera shirt to a business meeting or wedding would be considered perfectly formal and appropriate male attire. In 2010, Cuba actually declared the guayabera to be its "official formal dress garment."[2] During the time that I lived in the Dominican Republic—another place where guyaberas are worn—I came to realize that the guayabera was the equivalent of wearing a suit in many other parts of the world. And while people tend to think that wearing any kind of suit is generally a safe bet, differences in details can be laden with particular messages. In Italy, for example, brightly colored business shirts and ties are appreciated as fashionable, but in Japan anything but a classic white button-down could potentially be perceived as unprofessional.

Fortunately, all you really need to know is that the notion of being formally dressed is a moving target, and when you cross cultures you can't assume that people "read" clothing the same way you do. To err on the side of caution, try not to make assumptions even within your own country, because every company, community, and region may have its own set of formality standards and perceptions.

I'm never shy about asking my clients what to wear when I'm preparing to lead a workshop at their company. While dressing in what I perceive to be a traditionally professional way may be vital for success in certain places, dressing this way in other places—like Silicon Valley's start-up arena—may cause you to lose credibility, because people might feel that you just don't get them.

Of course, dress is just one small aspect of the formality puzzle. If you are truly going to get familiar with your formality zone, you have to consider your gut reactions in a wide variety of situations. In the following self-assessment exercise, note your gut reaction to the formality level of the five common scenarios I describe. The exercise is merely a starting point to get you thinking about your associations with formality and informality so you can start to open your mind to other ways of perceiving them.

Find Your Formality Zone

Situation	Too Formal	Too Informal	Just Right
You get an email from a new colleague you've never met (someone of the same rank). She begins the email with "Hi [your first name]."			
You arrive at a small dinner party (adults only), and the host is using paper napkins and plastic cups.			
Someone gets up and makes an elaborate show of handing you a business card during a group meeting.			
One of your employees comes to a meeting with a potential client or customer wearing jeans and flip-flops.			
At an internal staff meeting, everyone stands up when you enter the room.			

For every situation—whether you marked it too formal, too informal, or just right—someone from another culture might have marked it differently. Although people from the same culture may also differ in their perceptions of formality and its implications, people from the same culture do tend to have similar reactions.

Once you begin to get familiar with your own preferences and behaviors, you'll also become more attuned to the ways that formality—and its association with rank—can impact our interactions in unexpected ways, increasing your ability to head off a culture crash like the following one.

A few years ago I worked with a global petroleum company that had relocated a group of employees from Ecuador to various cities in the United States. After a few months, Ecuadorians in several cities began reporting that their bosses did not seem confident or competent in their jobs, because they were always asking the employees for advice about what to do. Meanwhile, their U.S. bosses had some complaints about the way that the Ecuadorian employees always seemed to be waiting for the next task to be assigned rather than taking initiative to solve problems themselves. What was happening was that both the bosses and the employees thought they were being respectful of each other, but the message they intended to convey by their behaviors was being misinterpreted. The U.S. boss thought he was being inclusive and egalitarian by inviting his employees to be part of the decision making and problem solving process (an informal behavior). By not offering suggestions to the boss or jumping in to fix a problem, the Ecuadorians were showing deference to the boss's higher rank (a more formal behavior). The solution was to make all parties aware of how their expectations for rank and formality differed, and to have them all adjust their behaviors in order to meet on a middle ground. Once the Ecuadorians realized that in taking more initiative they would still be perceived as respectful, and it would even benefit their relationships with their bosses, they quickly began to do so. The bosses, in turn, felt less obliged to be inclusive and offered up more solutions of their own, but still remained open and receptive to any of the employees' ideas that were offered. As a result, the number of complaints from both sides diminished significantly.

Adjusting your behaviors in order to convey the right level of respect for rank is no small feat, especially because we can't assume that the behaviors we typically use to convey respect will mean the same thing to people in other cultures. When dining with others, for example, you may consider the seat of honor at a rectangular table to be at the head of the table or just to the right of the head, while in other cultures (like the Chinese) the place of honor is usually the seat in the center facing east or facing the entrance.[3] At business meetings in certain cultures, the ends of the table may be filled by those with the highest rank, while in other cultures these seats would be filled by the lowest-ranking individuals. Even the honorary seats in cars, taxis, and trains are subject to cultural interpretation.

It's tough to hit on exactly the right formula for expressing formality (or informality) and all of its implications in a culture that is not your own. Sometimes you may be able to ask questions ahead of time in order to head off a potential crash. Other times the only way to get it right is to notice the crash and then sort it out afterward, as the Ecuadorians did in the preceding story. If you are living or working in another culture, you can become more adept at knowing how and when to be formal or informal simply by being observant of these behaviors in others, doing your best to mirror them appropriately, and noticing how people respond to your behaviors. If you're working with someone from another culture on your home turf, hit the pause button and consider the intent behind their use—or lack—of formality before you write someone off for being too rigid or overly eager, too casual or disrespectful—or make any other judgments that could impact your relationship.

Despite the variables, I generally err on the side of being formal when interacting with people from other cultures (based on the protocols of my own culture), because the general intentions behind many formal gestures are often understood. It's also always better to appear overly respectful than to risk being disrespectful. Starting with formality and adjusting for informality is also the best path when it comes to verbal and written exchanges, how to dress, and other forms of etiquette.

In the next section we take a closer look at the key roles played by formality and informality in certain aspects of work and daily life, and how to navigate the differences when crossing cultures.

Space Invaders: Respect for Place

Formality is used to show respect not only for people but also for the places that people inhabit, including sacred, public, and more intimate spaces. Most of us know that a certain level of formality is generally expected as a show of respect when entering religious and other sacred spaces, but how we demonstrate that respect varies across cultures. It could be a matter of dress code (like removal or addition of a head covering), how loudly you speak, how you walk, or how you hold your gaze. The best course of action when entering a sacred space is to follow the lead of others and be aware that there may be gender-specific expectations. If no one else is around, rely on your own rules of formal etiquette until someone else arrives and you can adjust as needed.

It can be tricky to navigate the formal-informal divide when you are visiting someone else's home. When guests visit my house, I always tell them to "make themselves at home." For me, that notion implies that my guests may sit where they like, relax the way they would in their own homes, and feel free to ask for anything they might need. Sometimes guests will ask for a tour of my home, and I am happy to oblige. I guide them through the various rooms of the house, including bathrooms and bedrooms—often dashing ahead to close the doors to messy closets. They often follow me into the kitchen and linger by the counter as I put the finishing touches on some appetizers or the meal. My approach and expectations reflect my informal programming, including a looseness about sharing some of the less-polished aspects of the meal and the more intimate aspects of my life.

Conversely, when I've been a guest at people's homes in more formal cultures, things unfold differently. In Colombia, for example, my family and I would usually be led to a room or area designated for the guests and shown where to sit. It would not be appropriate to request a tour of the more private rooms of the house, and the kitchen would often be considered off limits. In this context, formality is used as a way to keep others at a distance from the more intimate and unpolished aspects of their lives. This is not to say that all households in Colombia follow the same protocol—it can vary based on personal preferences, socioeconomics, and other factors—but there is a tendency to be more formal, just as there is a tendency for people from the United States to be less formal. Our conditioning in terms of formality in the home often begins at a very early age, which is why people often hold fast to these customs even when living in other cultures.

How do you expect guests to behave when entering your home? How about when you are a guest? Is it okay to put your feet up on a chair? If someone does this in your home, do you feel this is rude or does it imply that your guest is relaxed and happy? Does this change when you are in an office setting, store, or a restaurant? What about how other people's children behave in your home? Is it acceptable for them to run around and play as raucously as they please in certain rooms?

Perceptions and acceptability related to how we conduct ourselves in certain spaces can vary widely across and within cultures. What might be perceived as a slight lack of respect for someone's home in one culture could be seen as a major affront by others. This is exactly the kind of offense that a U.S.-trained Iraqi force deftly avoided in 2009, when they canceled a planned raid on a suspected weapons cache because it was raining. "It was absolutely the right call," said the American captain quoted in a *New York Times* article. He explained that the raid would have required soldiers to traipse through people's houses during a rainstorm in muddy boots. Tracking mud into people's homes might have made more enemies than the troops arrested, because it would be construed as disrespectful—a concern that people from the U.S. might have considered secondary to the task at hand. "It's not the way we're used to doing things, but it has become the way we're used to doing things," the captain said. The author of the article goes on: "Across such cultural differences, the Iraqis learn from the Americans and the Americans learn from the Iraqis, imperfectly and only within limits. And still the training continues, with both sides complying on some points and pushing back on others."[4]

It's a lesson that speaks to the need for us as individuals to adjust behaviors as needed (to the best of our ability) in the interest of reducing conflict and displaying respect. But this story also highlights that it's not a one-way street, and we can hope to truly avoid culture crashes only if both parties are self-aware and open to seeing things from a new perspective.

"Call Me Bob": The Importance of Titles

According to the unwritten rules of Swiss etiquette, a person should always refer to a more senior counterpart at work as Mr. or Ms. (*Herr* or *Frau*) until he or she gives you the green light to use each other's first names. A colleague of mine based in Basel, Switzerland, explained this to me, illustrating his assertion with a story about how it took eight years for his officemate to finally suggest that they move to a first-name basis. It wasn't as if they hadn't gotten to know each other—they were literally sharing a small office.

While waiting eight years to call someone by their first name might be a bit extreme (even for the Swiss), consider that in countries like Japan, China, and South Korea, first names are seldom used in the workplace. People who have been working together for years may not even know each other's first names. On the opposite end of the spectrum is the United States, where people are quick to say "Call me Bob," often while they are still shaking hands for the very first time.

When my daughter's seven-year-old friends call me Mr. Landers, I actually cringe a little. To my ear, it suggests that the person addressing me thinks I'm old, stuffy, and uptight—that I'm not as free-spirited and cool as I think I am (or aspire to be). I usually ask them to call me Michael, but some kids just don't feel comfortable doing this, because their parents have clearly told them that they must use this formal title when addressing adults as a show of respect for my seniority.

On the other hand, in some situations I do think a formal title is essential. For example, when I am writing an email to someone I don't know, I always use the more formal "Mr." or "Ms." If the person responds and signs using their first name, then I also switch to their first name. But these days, many people don't bother with titles in emails, even when reaching out for the first time. Part of the reason is that emails (and texts or social media messages) are generally perceived as a quicker, more informal way of communicating—as opposed to calling on the phone or writing letters. But don't let the format fool you. The person on the receiving end of the email may not differentiate the same way you do between all of these modes of communication, and you may be starting off on the wrong foot by being too casual in your use of title—and even in the way you close out the letter.

Why do some cultures tend to use formal titles more often or for longer periods of time than others? The reasons vary from culture to culture, but one major factor is the value that a particular culture places on hierarchy, as noted at the start of this chapter. In places where the societal organization hinges on having a well-defined sense of hierarchy, the use of formal titles helps to maintain and reinforce the social strata. It also lets others know when someone has made a leap (gaining social status) or a fall to another level. The titles serve as signposts to help you navigate the social hierarchy, letting you know how you should interact with someone and vice versa, so that nobody's feathers get ruffled and the social order is maintained.

I've recruited people from certain countries who refused to accept job offers because the company wouldn't offer them more formal titles, even though the money and responsibility were in line with what they wanted. In societies where class and status play a major role at work and in everyday lives, formal titles are an important form of social capital and are often nonnegotiable. Conversely, there are other countries that tend to shun social hierarchy for historical or sociopolitical reasons, along with the formal titles and behaviors that support it. Although these hierarchies exist in more informal societies (such as the United States, Australia, Israel, and Sweden), people often downplay their seniority in an effort to reflect their own ideologies. In these cultures, it's the *lack* of formal titles that may be used to reinforce a social order that hinges on ideals like equality.

A current trend among U.S. companies is to do away with business titles altogether, suggesting that everyone is an equally important member of the team. Although employees of these companies may still have clearly defined roles, official titles are rarely acknowledged internally or externally. In some companies, even senior staff members have business cards with just the person's name and department. These days, it's not unusual for people in the United States to arrive at a meeting without any kind of business card. Who needs business cards when people can get all your contact information and even your full work history on networking sites like LinkedIn? Although business cards are still preferable in many industries, people are becoming increasingly comfortable sending links to their profile page if they've forgotten their cards.

This *in*formality around business titles and cards is intended to flatten any sense of hierarchy, even if the notion is more aspirational than authentic. But several of these "flattened" companies are starting to rethink this strategy in their overseas offices, where the lack of titles can be detrimental to winning business, establishing credibility and relationships, or simply being respected.

For people from countries that are organized around strong social hierarchies, like South Korea, Japan, and Taiwan, the lack of titles can cause great confusion. Without knowledge of someone's rank, they don't know how to respectfully interact with the person—and they might prefer to just walk away rather than risk any impropriety. Showing up at a meeting without a business card—or with a card lacking a title—can seriously derail relationship-building efforts. It's almost the equivalent of refusing to shake hands at a Western business meeting.

But even if you did arrive bearing a business card with a title, you still might be in for a culture crash. That's because it's not just about whether you hand over a card or what it says, but how you do it.

Tiny Ceremonies

Another way formality is often expressed is through ceremony: an elaborate display of actions that imply respect for a person, object, place, or tradition. In cultures that tend toward informality, the notion of ceremony is mostly affiliated with special occasions like weddings and graduations. But in cultures that tend be more formal, daily life can be filled with tiny ceremonies used to convey important messages.

Let's return to business cards. Have you ever been at one of those meetings where people distribute business cards like dealers at a blackjack table? I'm often tempted to say "Hit me again" before even looking at the card. Have you ever considered how *you* usually deliver a business card? And what about how you receive a card: do you examine it closely or glance at it quickly before stuffing it in your pocket? At a big meeting, have you ever stacked and shuffled the pile of cards you received—another unwitting nod to your inner croupier?

While tossing your cards on the table and sticking received cards in your pocket may be de rigueur at meetings in some countries, it could get you into trouble with people who hail from places where the etiquette for giving and getting business cards is full of hidden messages. Although every culture will abide by its own set of distinct guidelines, in more formal cultures people generally stand up to deliver cards individually, no matter how many people are sitting around the table. And when the cards are presented, it's usually with both hands and the information facing your counterpart. It's expected that the receiver will study the card—possibly commenting on a logo or title—before carefully placing it on the table until the end of the meeting, or in a special card case, suggesting that it is being handled with care. Then the tiny business card ceremony is complete, and everyone feels respected.

When exchanging business cards across cultures, your best bet is to err on the side of being more formal and avoid stuffing, stacking, or jotting notes on the back of someone's business card.

Eating and Drinking

The way we eat and drink is highly influenced by our cultural programming, and often relates to differences in formality expectations. Being aware of how you eat and drink is particularly important because sharing meals is often one of the main ways that we build relationships with others. But sizing up formality levels associated with food and drink can be tricky business, because each culture makes its own rules about what constitutes formal or "proper" etiquette in this context. For example, when someone burps during or after a meal in the United States, it's considered impolite and too casual, even if the meal itself is considered very informal. In parts of China and Bahrain, however, burping is considered good manners. Other simple actions—like slurping, how we hold our knives, or how much food we leave uneaten on our plates—all come with implicit messages that can vary across cultures. But differences in basic table manners are just the tip of the iceberg when it comes to understanding the role that formality plays in how we eat and drink—and most important, how we break bread in an effort to build relations with others.

As an example, think about how you pour an alcoholic drink. In the United States, only bartenders and connoisseurs tend to pay attention to how a drink is poured into a glass. For many Japanese people, however, pouring is a careful and ritualistic ceremony that most people learn and perform when drinking with others. The first few times I went out for after-work drinks with Japanese colleagues, I marveled at the way they ceremoniously filled my beer glass. No matter who was doing the pouring, the person would carefully hold the beer bottle in two hands, filling my glass so the beer reached the highest point possible without spilling. I was expected to lift and hold my glass with two hands at an angle to imbibe the liquid.

During my time in Japan I learned that it was preferable to avoid pouring anything into my own glass, because it could be construed as a selfish act. And this applies not only to alcohol but to other kinds of drinks too. The rules of proper etiquette dictated that I fill others' glasses first, with hope that they would get the message that I also wanted them to refill mine (nonverbal communication at play). If women are present, it's often expected that they do the pouring instead of men. As one blogger aptly put it, "It's generally considered feminine charm to pour drinks for people. Women are most likely to pour drinks. This is engrained into Japanese culture much the way men opening doors for women is engrained into several European cultures."[5]

Even after living there for several years, I was still struck by how unnecessarily elaborate it all seemed to me in contrast to the mostly thoughtless pours that I had been doling out and receiving most of my life. Although I did adapt to the Japanese way of pouring, occasionally I would unwittingly revert to my native habits. My colleagues were never visibly offended by my faux pas, but I did notice that I received very positive reactions when I played by their more ceremonious rules.

Rituals around drinking vary from country to country, and it depends on what and where you are drinking. For example, when you are invited to a Jordanian home, the host will usually offer you a type of Arabic coffee called *gahuwa murra* served piping hot in a very small amount in a very small cup. The coffee is served first to whoever is on the right, and on from there. The coffee is expected to be finished in about four or five sips so that it remains hot. If you hand the cup back to the host, you will automatically be given another cup. Three cups is the traditional limit, but if you have had enough after one cup, you are supposed to shake the empty cup back and forth from right to left two to four times before handing it to your host. If you don't drink your first cup of coffee, it can suggest to the host that you have come to ask for something—like a favor. This is actually how some marriage proposals begin![6]

On the opposite end of the spectrum are the cultures in which a host would simply hand someone a mug of coffee (perhaps in a cup that says "#1 Dad" on it) and ask if they take it with milk or cream and/or sugar. The host might offer a refill after some time, but the guest would also feel free to request more if desired. No additional protocol, no other hidden messages. It's simply a cup of coffee.

When it comes to having coffee in a public place there are also notable differences in formality or ceremony across cultures. In Italy, for example, many people go to coffee bars for their morning fix. No matter how rushed people are, they stand or sit at the bar, where they are handed a ceramic cup filled with their steaming elixir of choice, accompanied by a saucer and tiny metal spoon. The options are usually limited to items like a café americano, caffe latte, espresso, or cappuccino (but not after 11 A.M. and never after a meal).[7] People take a few moments to enjoy their coffee, perhaps have a quick chat with other patrons or the barista, pay, and get on with their day.

In the United States, the equivalent to the Italian coffee bar are coffee shop chains like Starbucks, where customers can choose from 87,000 different drink combinations offered throughout the seasons.[8] No matter which coffee you choose, the experience of buying and drinking it is much less ceremonious than the experience in a typical Italian coffee bar. Ironically, the founder of the Starbucks chain, Howard Schultz, originally designed the experience to be similar to the Italian experience.[9] But over time, U.S. culture seems to have transformed it, stripping the experience of formalities and creating an assembly line–like feel that gets people out the door at maximum speed. In most Starbucks there are only paper cups and plastic stirrers as opposed to ceramics and silverware, there's not much chatting with the barista (too busy) or others, and people most often drink their coffee on the go rather than on-site. The process of getting coffee in the

United States is still a ritual, but it is a very informal one compared to the Italian ritual. Many people in the United States love Starbucks precisely because of the way that the experience gets them in and out quickly, without any formalities that might be deemed fussy. For Italians, the "fuss" is an integral part of the process.

The practice of more formal rituals often requires more time to perform, which is why fast-food places do away with them. According to Eric Schlosser, the author of *Fast Food Nation*, at least one in four people in the United States eat some type of fast food every day[10]—a statistic that speaks to not only the way people in the United States value efficiency, but also how little formality matters. Most offerings at fast-food places can be eaten with your hands, from burgers and sandwiches, to fries and chips, to ice cream cones. Drinks are self-serve; you carry you own food on a plastic tray and dump your trash when you are done. Almost everything is disposable (plates, cutlery, cups), and the décor includes tables and plastic-coated seats that can be wiped down with a sponge in a single pass.

To date, the number-one fast-food restaurant in the United States is McDonald's.[11] It's also achieved varying levels of success in some 118 countries.[12] When the Golden Arches first debuted in some of the more formal cultures, they struggled to survive after the novelty had worn off. Although McDonald's' original policy was to not adapt to preferences of foreign cultures, they eventually realized that they had to make concessions to survive, in terms of both people's taste for certain foods and their taste for formality. It's a decision that has served them well over the years.

In France, McDonald's' number-two market, some of the restaurants have been made to look like bistros, with classy, spacious interiors, enticing patrons to linger over their meals.[13] Menu choices are tailored to regional palates and sometimes served on reusable tableware. When one franchisee from the city of Toulouse redesigned the interiors of his twelve restaurants, it resulted in a 20-percent uptick in sales.[14]

The way McDonald's found success by adapting to more formal tastes is an instructive example of how important it can be to adapt to varying preferences for formality when interacting with people from other cultures in our daily lives. When and if you adapt, it doesn't mean that your personal formality preferences have changed, or that you need to judge the merits of being more or less formal. It simply shows that you are acknowledging and respecting the preferences of those from other cultures.

This applies to not just how you run your fast-food franchise, but also how you present yourself—in other words, your personal "brand." Once you become more aware of the role that formality or informality plays in what you say, how you write, the way you dress, and so on, you can more easily make the slight shifts needed to have more successful interactions and build better connections across cultures.

In each of the preceding chapters we've explored distinct aspects of our cultural programming, including formality, views of time, verbal and nonverbal communication, and group and individual orientations. There are plenty of other aspects we could also explore, but in doing this work over the past twenty years, I've found that these are the topics that serve as the best primer for raising your level of self-awareness in a wide variety of contexts, and empowering you to assess and adjust your behavior in order to enhance your cross-cultural interactions.

There is, however, one more key step to laying the groundwork for enhanced cross-cultural agility: getting familiar with the all-encompassing ideologies that drive behaviors in each culture—including your own. These are sets of deep-rooted values that collectively shape the way people act, react, and interact in all types of situations. While you can certainly make great strides toward improving your cross-cultural interactions without knowing how all of these underlying forces affect you or others, it's only by exploring and understanding them that your ability to forge strong connections with people from a particular culture will truly soar.

CULTURE KEY

Quick Tips for Formal-Informal Crossings

Titles
It's best to start with appropriate titles and honorifics and stop using them only if or when your counterpart does the same or requests it.

Email
Always begin and end with the more formal salutations, such as "Dear (Title)" and "Sincerely," until your counterpart makes a move toward using more informal language.

Texts/Messaging
Avoid use of slang or acronyms like LMK ("let me know") unless the other person uses them. Better to avoid emoji completely, since they may relate to expressions that can be interpreted as disrespectful.

Dress
Find out the dress code before a meeting or function. When that's not possible, err on the side of formality. It's easier to remove a formal article of clothing like a jacket, tie, or jewelry than to add something.

Business Cards
Start by being more formal: hand your card to someone with information facing them, using two hands if possible (if not just your right hand). Also, try to receive a card with both hands. Take time to look at the card before putting it down, and keep the card on the table until the end of your meeting, or put it somewhere "safe" as if it were a treasured object.

Drinking and Eating
Observe and mirror the behaviors of others when it comes to using the correct utensils, what to eat and drink and when, how much or how little to leave on your plate, who pours a drink for whom, and so on.

SEVEN

Core Values

Taking your cultural awareness
to the next level

I am a TCK. Chances are you've never heard that term before. But you probably know other TCKs. They are everywhere. Barack Obama is one. So are Uma Thurman, Kobe Bryant, and the late Freddie Mercury. You might actually be one yourself. Don't worry—it's not contagious, although it has been known to cause identity crises.

TCK is short for "third culture kid." It's a term coined in the 1950s by sociologist Ruth Hill Useem and neatly explained by another sociologist named David C. Pollock: "A Third Culture Kid (TCK) is a person who has spent a significant part of his or her developmental years outside the parents' culture. The TCK frequently builds relationships to all of the cultures, while not having full ownership in any. Although elements from each culture may be assimilated into the TCK's life experience, the sense of belonging is in relationship to others of similar background."[1]

Today, the acronym is sometimes modified to ATCK (adult third culture kid) to include people who have been deeply affected by multiple cultures as adults. As I mentioned in the introduction, an estimated 244 million people currently live outside their country of origin—a number that will undoubtedly continue grow in the wake of factors such as increased migration and economic globalization.[2]

TCKs of all ages often reveal themselves in the way that they answer the question, "Where are you from?" I always have trouble with this question. My quick answer is that I was born in Boston but raised overseas. The real answer traces my journey from my birth in the United States to American parents, spending my school years in Colombia, Brazil, and the Dominican Republic, but returning to Boston every summer. I also spent my early twenties in Japan before settling again in the United States.

I identify culturally with all of these places where I lived in my younger years, but in a way that highlights my perpetual identity crisis. When I'm in Spanish-speaking countries throughout Latin America, I often say that I am gringo (from the United States) on the outside but Latino on the inside. My tendencies are a mash-up of the programming I picked up from the various cultures in which I lived. But mostly, I'm a chameleon with a deep-rooted instinct to adapt as quickly as possible to the ways of those around me.

Despite occasional bouts of identity confusion, being a TCK does have some benefits, and it plays an important role in the work that I do. For starters, it has afforded me a perspective of certain cultures that I would not have if I'd spent the entirety of my youth in the same place. Being a TCK has made me acutely aware of some of the underlying differences that go far beyond issues like punctuality or table manners. I'm talking about a set of integral ideologies that I call *core values*, which shape the way we live our lives. This set of core values is the collective force that drives many of those tendencies that we've touched on in the book: group versus individual orientation, direct versus indirect, formal versus informal, limited time versus unlimited time, and so on. Some of your core values will be truly your own, having evolved from personal experience and biology, but many will be a result of your cultural programming. Tapping into your core cultural values can offer a kind of enlightenment that is essential to not only building successful relations, but also sustaining them.

Not unlike being fluent in another language, developing a deep understanding of the core values of another culture (and how they are expressed) will exponentially enhance your ability to communicate effectively, intuit hidden messages, and establish deep and enduring connections.

The core value concept was first introduced to me by one of my favorite grad school professors, cross-cultural expert L. Robert Kohls. In 1984, Kohls published a short paper titled *The Values Americans Live By*, in which he proposed that there are thirteen core values that dictate behaviors in the United States.[3] Those values include things like equality, individualism and privacy, practicality and efficiency. While it's interesting to ponder his complete list of core American values, what was more eye-opening for me was his assessment of how important it is to be familiar with these values if you are trying to build a connection with someone from the United States

In one passage, he writes "if foreign visitors really understand how deeply ingrained these 13 values are in Americans, they will be able to understand 95% of American actions, actions which might otherwise appear 'strange,' 'confusing' or 'unbelievable' when evaluated from the perspective of the foreigner's own society and its values."[4]

I also gleaned from this statement that those actions that we perceive as strange, confusing, frustrating, or downright shocking are actually clues we can use to unearth the most deeply rooted and pervasive values of a culture. As a TCK, it was something that I had known subconsciously for years, but it wasn't until I saw it on paper that I began to consciously use these clues to decipher other people's behaviors and their underlying values.

These days, nary a work day goes by without clients telling me what puzzles them or pisses them off about people from other cultures. When someone complains about one of my "home" cultures, I'm rarely offended, thanks to years of training myself to be objective no matter what culture it is, whether I'm listening to Brazilians discuss challenges with the Chinese, Germans with the Saudis, New Yorkers with people from L.A.—and even between the sales and engineering teams within the same company.

After years of listening to the diverse array of accusations and frustrations, it's become quite evident to me that Kohls' assertion is correct, and not just as it relates to people from the United States. The things that bother and perplex you about a specific person, group, or culture are often linked to the differences between your core values and someone else's.

For example, when I ask people from other cultures what annoys, puzzles, or frustrates them about people and businesses from the United States, I often get similar responses. Here are a few:

- Americans act friendly, but it seems superficial. They ask how you are doing, but they don't have time to hear the real answer. They disclose personal details about their lives, which suggests that they want to develop the relationship further, but the next time we meet they are distant.

- Why are there so many options at supermarkets and restaurants? Fifty kinds of cereal, dozens of drink options, ten salad dressing options? It's exhausting and overwhelming.

- When I visit someone's home in the United States, the host often offers to take you on a tour. They even show the bathrooms, the bedrooms, and the closets, which feels inappropriate. Why would they think that we would want to see all the rooms in their home?

People from the United States behave this way largely based on their core values. And people are annoyed, puzzled, or frustrated by these behaviors because they are so different from their own. Here is how I connect the dots between these complaints and some of the core U.S. values:

Americans appear and act friendly, but it seems superficial.
(Values: *informality, individualism, equality*)

Americans tend to be very open when it comes to disclosing personal details with people they don't know that well. This speaks to individualism (*let me tell you about me*), informality (*no need for protocol here; let's just be ourselves*) or equality (*we are on same level—I am going to be as friendly and engaged with you as I would with anyone else*).

Why so many options at markets and restaurants? It's overwhelming.
(Values: *equality, individualism, immediate gratification*)

Most people in the United States take pride in the notion of living in the land of opportunity and options. In this diverse nation, people strive to cater to as many individual needs or preferences as possible—and to be equal opportunity providers (*no one should feel left out or underserved*). People also want to know they can get what they want anywhere, any time.

Why would they think that we want to see all the rooms in their home?
(Values: *equality, individualism, informality*)

In the United States, people's homes are often a reflection of their individuality, and they want to be appreciated for it. Having no rooms designated as off limits underscores the informality of the experience—there's no shame in seeing behind-the-scenes kitchen prep, messy kids' room, and so on. The home tour is also a means of highlighting equality: *I am happy to show you what I have, and it's yours to enjoy while you are here.*

In my opinion, the four values that I call out in these examples—equality, individualism, informality, and immediate gratification—are among the clearest and most pervasive core values that drive behaviors in the United States. If you are from the United States, chances are you perceive these values as basic and universally understood human rights, not values unique to U.S. culture. While it's true that many other cultures value the rights and freedoms associated with equality and individualism to varying degrees, the perceptions and expectations of these ideologies can drive behaviors in very different ways.

In other cultures, an ideology like equality may not be valued as highly and may have less of an impact on people's behaviors and the choices they make. The top spot held by equality in the United States might be replaced by a contrasting ideology, such as group welfare. In Table 7.1, lists some of Kohls' contrasts. It shows his list of the thirteen core U.S. values plotted alongside their counterparts in other cultures.[5]

Kohls' thirteen values are just one take on what makes Americans tick—as is his list of contrasting values. Other scholars have their own take. Like anything in sociology, it's open to interpretation. But the chart provides a valuable starting point from which you can begin to assess your own core values and develop the skills you need to begin to uncover them in other cultures.

A VALUES COMPARISON

U.S. Values	Some Other Countries' Values
Control over the environment	Fate
Change	Tradition
Time & its control	Human interaction
Equality	Hierarchy/rank/status
Individualism/privacy	Group's welfare
Self-help	Birthright inheritance
Competition	Cooperation
Future orientation	Past orientation
Action/work orientation	"Being" orientation
Informality	Formality
Directness/openness/honesty	Indirectness/ritual/"face"
Practicality/efficiency	Idealism
Materialism/acquisitiveness	Spiritualism/detachment

Table 7.1: Kohls' thirteen values

Core Values in Action

Identifying core values is tougher than you might expect. There are clues and patterns that you can learn to spot, but the core values of someone from another culture are less likely to reveal themselves until you get familiar with your own. Core values play out in countless aspects of our work and personal lives, but it's hard to recognize them unless you know what you are looking for. To help prime your mind to recognize them, it's helpful to consider how core values ultimately impacted the success of two different products in the following examples.

When it comes to marketing across cultures, success often hinges on whether or not the plan has tapped into the core cultural values of the target customer. When marketing strategies miss the target, they fail—as the supermarket chain Fresh & Easy did. In December 2012, Fresh & Easy announced plans to pull out of all U.S. operations. Owned and operated by Tesco, the second-largest retailer in the world and the grocery market leader in the U.K., the brand just hadn't caught on after five years, so its two hundred U.S. stores were either shuttered or sold off. When the company went down, dozens of business analysts pontificated on the reasons for its demise, most of them citing a lack of cultural awareness. Essentially, the company lacked an understanding of how U.S. core values affect consumer expectations, and how these can shift depending on the context.[6] Let's examine a few of the company's missteps more specifically:

- The markets prided themselves on not offering traditional coupons, which are seen as a sign of desperation in the U.K.[7] But coupons are not perceived this way in the United States, where equality rules the day. Many Americans love clipping coupons and getting a deal, no matter how wealthy they are.

- Vegetables were mostly wrapped in clear plastic, an attempt to play to American's preference for expedience and food safety.

But depriving people of the chance to inspect the produce and make their own selections was disempowering.[8]

- An expert, quoted in the *Los Angeles Times*, said that part of the reason for the brand's failure was that it didn't customize inventory based on what shoppers liked.[9] They didn't play to the individualism value. The selection was also limited, so there wasn't always something to suit everyone's tastes.

- Fresh & Easy didn't sell goods in bulk, since people in the U.K. tend to shop multiple times a week and often have relatively small fridges. They failed to acknowledge that in the U.S. people like to be able to economize in terms of both cost and trips to the market, and for many, filling a cavernous refrigerator correlates with the American self-image of prosperity.[10]

- The store relied solely on self-checkout scanners, as they do in the U.K. They may have assumed that people in the United States would appreciate this, since they place such a high value on self-reliance and all things DIY (do it yourself). But U.S. shoppers often prefer assistance when it comes to scanning the prices of the dozens of items in their carts.[11] Self-checkout stations may take longer than being helped by a human cashier. People from the United States also tend to prefer human interaction in supermarkets, which they view as community hubs.

The notion that a supermarket serves as a community hub was perhaps Fresh & Easy's most glaring oversight. Early advertising made people think Fresh & Easy would rival Trader Joe's, a highly successful specialty market found across the United States. Trader Joe's was described by the *Guardian* as "a sophisticated but simple chain which markets a warm and fuzzy feeling to customers with relaxing music, 'trading post' decor, an emphasis on organic food, community involvement and even in-store competitions for children."[12] While

Trader Joe's misses the mark in some ways too (they also shrink-wrap some produce), the market's overall vibe plays to the American desire for the supermarket experience to feel like a community-building activity, not unlike going to a neighborhood market or a church.

As a result of Fresh & Easy's cultural misadventure, the parent company lost almost $2 billion. According to one industry analyst, "Tesco's failure will rank as one of the biggest among food retailers in modern supermarket history."[13]

Although the stakes are not this high for most people endeavoring to build businesses or relations in a multicultural arena, failure to thoroughly investigate core values and associated expectations can completely derail their efforts. More importantly for most of us, Fresh & Easy provides a cautionary case study for contemplating how our values can color our expectations in places like supermarkets or anywhere else that we spend time. We all have expectations of these places, whether we realize it or not. The same goes for activities and objects. Whether it's a supermarket, a car, or an office holiday party, our perceptions of these things are influenced by our core values, which are very often tough to discern through simple observation.

The other example I'll share in order to prime your brain to recognize core values concerns one of the most globally beloved products: Lego. In his bestselling book *The Culture Code*, psychoanalyst and author Clotaire Rapaille explores Legos (among other things) as examples of cultural ideologies or "codes" that are reflected in various products and activities. He describes these codes as being unconsciously acquired through emotional experiences that leave their mark on us as we grow up. The codes vary from culture to culture, and they shape how we behave as consumers. He says that knowing the code is the key to successfully marketing and selling anything in a particular culture.[14]

Based on this concept, Rapaille deciphers the code for food in the United States as "fuel," while in France he says it's associated with "pleasure," and in Japan with "perfection." He also makes the case that people in the United States associate Jeeps with horses (pioneering the open road) and toilet paper with independence (harkening back to those first days of parent-free wiping).[15] But it's his analysis of the Danish Legos that really drives home the idea that we all have different expectations and ways of interacting as a result of our cultural codes, which are related to core values. Here's an excerpt from Rapaille's book about it:

> Lego, the Danish toy company, found instant success with their interlocking blocks in the German market ... Why? ... German children opened a box of Legos, sought out the instructions, read them carefully, and then sorted the pieces by color. They began building, comparing their assembly progress to the crisp, helpful illustrations in the instruction booklet. When they were finished, they had an exact duplicate of the product shown on the cover of the box. They showed it to Mother who clapped approvingly and put the model on a shelf. *Now the children needed another box.*
>
> Without knowing it, Lego had tapped into the Culture Code for Germany itself: ORDER.[16]

Rapaille contrasts this with how U.S. kids interact with Legos:

> American children could not have cared less. They would tear into the boxes, glance fleetingly at the instructions (if they looked at them at all), and immediately set out on a construction project on their own. They seemed to be having a wonderful time, but they were as likely to build, say, a fort, as they were to build the automobile for which the blocks were intended. And when they were done, they would tear their fort apart and start over from scratch. To Lego's dismay, a single box of Legos could last for years.[17]

Although Lego sets have long been extremely popular in the United States, sales per capita were lower than expected because of the way that each set was—and is—perpetually reused. Although Rapaille doesn't say this exactly, here is my assessment of why U.S. kids didn't just make what they saw in the picture:

- They preferred to express their individual creativity than copy the model.

- They didn't bother to read the instructions or follow the illustrations, because they wanted immediate gratification.

- They were not driven by the goal of formally displaying their work, because they preferred informality.

The lesson in this Lego tale is applicable not just to product designers and marketers, but also to people working in almost any industry that is trying to engage a group of multicultural users. The insights offered by the Fresh & Easy and Lego cases also have bearing on our personal lives, opening our minds to and exemplifying the pervasive impact that these core values can have on our preferences and expectations for everything from architectural design, to organizing meetings, to how we celebrate birthdays.

Uncovering Core Values (and Putting Them to Work for You)

Now is a good time to pause and contemplate your own set of core values and how they drive your perceptions and preferences. What beliefs do you live by? What are the guiding principles that help you define your expectations of activities, places, things, and people? Most of us can rattle off a few—probably a mix of national and personal values that we've cultivated through our life experiences. But there are always values so deeply embedded in our psyches that we don't ever question how they got there. They may be based on national values that have taken root so long ago that the original need or desire that spawned them is no longer relevant to our lives—yet we live by them anyway.

To get started on your self-investigation, it may be helpful to refer back to Kohls' chart in Table 7.1 and consider how the values in either column may or may not resonate with you, paying close attention to those values that you may have thought of as universal—perhaps values like equality, individuality, the importance of tradition, or the role of fate. Think about how some of these values relate to your own expectations and behaviors when it comes to things like shopping, choosing where to live, running a business, or interacting with people of other genders.

To gain more insight into their own sets of core values, my clients also find it helpful to contemplate the "why" behind this series of simple questions. The answers won't tell you everything you need to know about your values, but they reflect the kinds of questions you should be continually asking yourself in order to become more aware of the major motivating factors in your life.

- *People:* Think about the people in your life now and in the past. Who do you really connect with? Who do you merely tolerate? Who pushes your buttons? Who do you respect?

- *Places:* Think about the places you have lived or visited. Which ones would you move to in a heartbeat? Which ones did you want to leave right away? What about the places you have worked or studied? What were your best and worst experiences—and why?

- *Things:* What is a product or service that you really enjoy and come back to again and again? Why do you like it? How about the ones that just don't work for you, or the ones that you despise?

If you take the time to truly contemplate all of this, you will start to notice patterns. Certain values will show up for you in a wide variety of scenarios. You can also start discerning if your values are culturally influenced (as opposed to just being a personal value) by paying attention to what behaviors are generally encouraged, appreciated, and rewarded by others as opposed to those that are not. Which actions are repeatedly encouraged by your peers at work, your friends, your family, and anyone else with whom you regularly interact?

These are exactly the same cues that will enable you to uncover the core values of someone from another culture. In your interactions with a particular person, which behaviors do you notice them encouraging or discouraging? What behaviors are appreciated or unappreciated? Think about whether you have observed similar reactions by other people (or groups of people) from that same culture. If a pattern becomes apparent, chances are you have identified a core value.

Once you've identified a particular value or set of values, you can anticipate how it might play out in different scenarios and stave off a potential culture crash. For example, if you are someone who believes you are in control of your environment, and you are working with people who believe that fate is in control, you can prepare yourself by loosening your expectations about meeting deadlines and sticking with prearranged plans. You would also be wise to adjust the way you exert influence, knowing that others are less likely to respond to a sense of urgency.

At the very least, armed with an awareness of your own core values, you will be better equipped to make wise decisions about where you work or the communities in which you spend your time. Just like individual countries, each company, organization, and community has its own subculture and a set of core values that drives behaviors and expectations. And you need to be able to understand these values and jibe with them in order to flourish there.

Finding a Good Fit: Organizational Values

A pioneer in the field of creative strategizing, the San Francisco–based design firm IDEO has been widely recognized for how they have helped businesses and organizations innovate in ingenious ways. They've helped rethink and improve everything from TSA security checkpoints, to customer savings programs at banks, to school lunch programs in urban areas. Under their guidance, Apple designed their first mouse, Intercell developed needle-free vaccines, Kaiser Permanente reorganized their nursing shifts, and Procter & Gamble built a better potato chip—to name just a few examples. As described in an article by *Fast Company* magazine, IDEO "has, in short, become the go-to firm for both American and foreign companies looking to cure their innovation anemia."[18]

With over five hundred employees and offices on three continents, IDEO chalks up most of their achievements to "design thinking"—a methodology they popularized that enables people to free up their way of thinking in the interest of developing innovative, human-centered solutions. But in truth, it's more than a working method for IDEO: it is the ultimate goal around which a set of core values has been crafted to yield success. Although I have not personally worked at this company, I know that these values are listed in a small red handbook given to every employee when he or she begins working there. Here is what IDEO CEO Tim Brown wrote about the impetus to create this book in 2014: "Clients often ask me how we built IDEO's creative culture. For 20 years, I did a lot of hand-waving and gave vague answers. Then, about a year ago, we decided we really should put our values in writing. The result was a slim hardcover called *The Little Book of IDEO*. In it, we distilled what makes our workplace tick into 7 human-centered axioms ..."[19]

The values—or axioms, as he calls them—can also be seen on the wall as soon as you enter into the San Francisco headquarters.[20] They include:

- Be optimistic

- Collaborate

- Embrace ambiguity

- Learn from failure
- Make others feel successful
- Take ownership
- Talk less, do more

These values are essentially a set of operating instructions for surviving and flourishing in the IDEO culture. Although Brown only recently codified them, these values originated in his brain decades ago as a set of behaviors and ways of thinking that enabled him to maximize his ability to conjure up innovative solutions for his clients. The more success these behaviors and ideologies yielded, the more *valuable* they became. Over the years, that set of values has probably evolved to optimize results in various contexts, as the scope and breadth of the company's projects expanded. Under Brown's leadership, the company grew—and continues to grow—by hiring and partnering with others who are willing to embrace these values that form the foundation of IDEO's company culture.

IDEO's core values took root and evolved the same way that national values do: inspired by the shared needs or wants of a group of people and fueled by a desire to flourish. The formation of IDEO's values was driven by a desire to succeed in business, whereas national values are often inspired by some other impetus—like the desire for equality by a group that has been denied it, or the need to live in harmony with others in a densely populated area.

Besides providing a set of guiding principles to succeed at work, IDEO's values define its office culture, like the way that the staff is organized and interacts with each other, and even the design of the workspaces, which are perpetually being redesigned to improve functionality. So imagine if you are someone who comes to work at IDEO and you just don't connect with that culture. Knowing the core values makes it easier to pinpoint why it just doesn't feel right. Maybe you are someone who flourishes in a more stable environment, where change is not a constant. Perhaps it's simply that you are someone who likes to work independently—or who is not comfortable with prolonged ambiguity. There could be any number of reasons.

The reasons that you mesh or don't mesh with IDEO or any other organizational culture can tell you a lot about your personal culture. But it can also tell you about your national culture. Regardless of how customized the value systems are in any one organizational subculture, they also tend to evolve in a way that is influenced by the deeply rooted national values of the geographic origin of the group or its founders.

Social networking platforms also provide excellent examples of the way that national culture pervades subcultures. Consider Facebook, for example: a virtual community that has all the hallmarks of a subculture. In order to flourish on Facebook, the user has to embrace the values on which the community was built, most of which are tied to U.S. values.

When Mark Zuckerberg created Facebook, he probably wasn't thinking about how he could tap into the United States' core values (unless trying to meet girls is one of them). Yet he tapped into many of them. Think about it:

- *Individualism*: Facebook allows you to tell the world what *you* are doing, reading, and thinking. It enables you to proclaim your distinct preferences and the individual choices you make daily. It allows users to shout "Look at me!"

- *Informality*: You can "friend" someone you haven't seen in thirty years without having to talk to them.

- *Equality*: Anybody can create a profile, and everyone's pages all use the same template.

- *Immediate gratification*: Take a photo of your food, post it, and receive comments before you take the first bite.

While Facebook is also successful in many other countries and cultures whose core values may differ from those of the United States, it's little wonder that the idea was spawned, developed, and executed in the United States by people raised in the United States.[21]

In his book *The Facebook Effect: The Inside Story of the Company That Is Connecting the World*, former *Fortune* magazine senior editor and technology expert David Kirkpatrick writes:

> But Zuckerberg's Facebook is resolutely American, even if it may not always seem so to its international users. Facebook's American-ness is revealed not because some Azerbaijan teenager meets a kid from Oklahoma, but by its intrinsic assumption about how people ought to behave. Zuckerberg's values reflect the liberties of American discourse. Facebook carries those values around the world, and that's having both positive and negative effects. In the United States, people take a certain amount of transparency and freedom of speech for granted but it comes at great cost in some other cultures.[22]

Of course, Facebook is beloved in many other countries too, but people in those cultures may utilize it differently. In some countries people prefer to use other social network platforms for various reasons, some of which are related to the freedoms that Kirkpatrick notes. Facebook is banned for political reasons in places like Iran, Egypt, Cuba, and China, which underscores differences in the core values of these governments.[23]

If Facebook adapted its platform in these countries, they would most likely find more success, although at a loss of the core values on which the very idea for Facebook was built. With other kinds of products and services, however, there is less at stake, making it easier to adjust them to mesh better with core values of certain cultures, like the way that McDonald's has adapted its style in France and other countries.

Of course, we can't all wait for these subcultures to bend to our values. More often than not, it's up to us as individuals to adjust to the organization with which we are working or interacting in order to build better relations with others, thus increasing the chances of both personal and group success. We all make assumptions about what behaviors will yield success in any group, based on our own set of core values and experiences. We unwittingly carry them with us into every group situation, where they define our actions and expectations—rising to a conscious level only when we are jarred by a culture crash. For example, imagine a new employee has just joined a U.S.-based company. The employee is relatively new to the United States, and this is how she is programmed to work:

- She defers to the group as much as possible.

- She rarely speaks about herself or calls attention to her achievements.

- She refers to everybody as Mr. or Ms.

- She always waits for those with a higher rank to tell her what to do and say.

- She takes her time to get things done and doesn't feel beholden to deadlines.

- She remains silent for a long period before responding to a question.

How long do you think this person will last in her new position? When I describe this scenario to employees at U.S.-based corporations during my workshops and ask them this question, their answer is usually "less than a week." Why? Largely because many of the behaviors this employee exhibited are completely counter to core U.S. values.

While the differences are usually most apparent when people move between national cultures, you don't have to come from another country to experience this kind of culture crash. Many of us have found ourselves in group cultures on our home turf that don't mesh with our own. Perhaps you find people are too direct or indirect, formal or informal, and so on. In my experience, this is one of the biggest reasons why people quit or are fired. When someone says "It just wasn't a good fit," sometimes it's just a euphemism, but other times it is directly related to differences in core values.

Your chances of being happy and being successful in an office or community subculture hinges on whether your core values mesh with theirs or you are willing to adjust them while you are immersed in the particular culture. There is no clear-cut path to identifying your personal set of core values—that elusive mix of national, organizational, and purely personal values that defines the way we perceive and move through the world—or anyone else's. Revelations about your core values may come when you least expect them. But there are clues and patterns to be found if you take the time to look for them, and great rewards to be reaped if you can remain mindful of them.

Unearthing your personal tapestry of core values is an ongoing endeavor. It's another part of the journey of self-discovery that you have embarked upon by reading this book and will hopefully continue throughout your life. Ultimately, the more you arm yourself with this kind of knowledge and self-awareness, the more empowered you will be to make smart decisions about how to navigate any kind of multicultural encounter.

CULTURE KEY

Quick Tips for Navigating Core Values

- Identify behaviors that are encouraged, appreciated, and rewarded as opposed to those that are discouraged, unappreciated, and looked down upon.

- Look for patterns: are there certain behaviors that appear repeatedly and in a variety of situations?

- Consider the meanings and values behind the behaviors.

- Adjust your expectations and behaviors based on the values you've uncovered in order to avoid a culture crash, to exert more influence on someone, or both.

Culture Crossings Past, Present, and Future

I n the last chapter we explored the unseen depths of our proverbial icebergs, in an attempt to understand how discrete values combine to inform the way we interact with the world around us. No single value is separate from our other values, and no behavior is unconnected to a value or perception. Much as ice crystals combine to give icebergs their shape, many kinds of cultural conditioning combine to shape our values and in turn our perceptions, thoughts, and behaviors.

At the very heart of our icebergs lies a seemingly universal tendency to stick to our own cultures and be wary of those that are different—a hardwired ethnocentrism that likely emerged as a survival instinct. There is no question that it is often easier, more comfortable, and safer to associate only with people who are more like us in the way they behave and think.

The ancient Greeks used the term *barbaros* to refer to foreigners, because when they spoke it sounded to the Greeks like an unintelligible "bar bar bar" babble. This is the origin of the English word "barbarian," a word and concept now used to denote people whom we perceive as uncivilized and savage. The Japanese often refer to foreigners as *gaijin*—"non-Japanese" or "alien"; in Hong Kong white foreigners are often referred to as *gweilo*, which literally means *ghost man*; in mainland China one may be *yáng guǐzi* or "foreign devil"; in Turkey it is *yabanci*, which has a root meaning of "uncivilized" and "savage"; and in Myanmar, for some it is *kalar* or "undesirable alien." Around the world, there are likely hundreds if not thousands of terms for foreigners, many with negative connotations.

But homogeneity no longer characterizes our communities and workplaces. Instead, we are defined by being part of a global era in which cities and countries are more diverse than ever. If your city, community, or work has not yet been touched by multiculturalism, chances are it will be soon. Places like South Orange, New Jersey— where more than fifty languages are spoken in the public schools—provide a snapshot of what many communities in the United States will soon look like. "For the first time, the next person you meet in this country—at work, in the library, at a coffee shop or a movie ticket line—will probably be of a different race or ethnic group than you," according to an in-depth study by *USA Today*.[1] Community portraits are diversifying elsewhere too, in countries like Canada, Germany, the United Kingdom, Russia, and many parts of the Middle East where immigration levels are climbing steadily.[2]

Business transactions everywhere also reflect new and greater diversity, especially as burgeoning economies in Asia, Latin America, and Africa continue to garner opportunities and expand into marketplaces well beyond their borders.

To consider these people as "foreign" is no longer accurate, nor is it in our best self-interest. They are our neighbors. They are our colleagues, clients, and customers. They are our teachers and fellow students. They have the potential to enrich our communities and workplaces in surprising ways. They can expand our way of thinking, teaching us things we never knew about ourselves, helping us to live more authentic lives. Their presence can lead us to develop a kind of self-awareness that can improve our ability to effectively communicate with anybody—even people from our own culture.

Being able to communicate effectively and build strong, sustainable connections with people from any culture is becoming an imperative for so many of us. It's something that cannot be achieved without being mindful of our own cultural programming and priming our minds to be receptive to new ways of thinking. This kind of mindfulness requires a form of brain training that will be easier for some than for others. But just like the rewards of physical or other kinds of conditioning, they will be worth the time and effort.

At the end of the book I've included a bibliography of additional reading so that you can continue your journey to greater cultural understanding, delving deeper into specific cultures and concepts. But even if your explorations end with this book, you now know that self-awareness is the key to successfully navigating a vast array of cross-cultural encounters. How you use the key is up to you, but it is undoubtedly the best way to open the door to peace and prosperity in the new global era.

NOTES

INTRODUCTION

1. Yoon Min-sik, "Netizens Abuzz over Gates's Handshake with President," *Korea Herald*, April 23, 2013, www.koreaherald.com/view.php?ud=20130423000714.

2. Tom Sheen, "Lionel Messi Offends Egypt with Boot Donation to Charity," *Independent–International*, March 30, 2016, www.independent.co.uk/sport/football/international/lionel-messi-offends-egypt-with-boot-donation-a6959531.html.

3. United Nations Population Fund, "Migration," May 23, 2016, www.unfpa.org/migration; Jeffrey S. Passel and D'Vera Cohn, "U.S. Population Projections: 2005–2050," Pew Research Center, February 11, 2008, accessed July 9, 2016, www.pewhispanic.org/2008/02/11/us-population-projections-2005-2050/.

4. Jie Zong and Jeanne Batalova, "Frequently Requested Statistics on Immigrants and Immigration in the United States," Migration Policy Institute, April 14, 2016, www.migrationpolicy.org/article/frequently-requested-statistics-immigrants-and-immigration-united-states.

5. Pew Research Center, "Chapter 5: U.S. Foreign-Born Population Trends," Modern Immigration Wave Brings 59 Million to U.S., Driving Population Growth and Change Through 2065, www.pewhispanic.org/2015/09/28/chapter-5-u-s-foreign-born-population-trends/

6. Pew Research Center, Modern Immigration Wave Brings 59 Million to U.S., Driving Population Growth and Change Through 2065: Views of Immigration's Impact on U.S. Society Mixed, September 28, 2015, www.pewhispanic.org/2015/09/28/modern-immigration-wave-brings-59-million-to-u-s-driving-population-growth-and-change-through-2065/. The period of growth projected is from 2015 to 2065.

7. U.S. Census Bureau Decennial Censuses, American Community Survey, and the Department of Homeland Security 2011.

8. Richard Florida, "America's Leading Immigrant Cities," *Atlantic*, CityLab, September 22, 2015, www.citylab.com/politics/2015/09/americas-leading-immigrant-cities/406438/.

9. Nicole Crowder, "Starting Over in Dearborn, Michigan: The Arab Capital of North America," *Washington Post*, March 5, 2015, www.washingtonpost.com/news/

in-sight/wp/2015/03/05/starting-over-in-dearborn-michigan-the-arab-capital-of-north-america/.

10. Wayne Drash, "In Iowa, Globalization and a Culture Clash," *CNN*, n.d., www.cnn .com/interactive/2015/07/us/culture-clash-american-story/.

11. Ibid.

12. Karen MacGregor, "International Students to Reach 3.8 Million by 2024," University World News, October 11, 2013, accessed July 11, 2016, www.universityworldnews .com/article.php?story=20131011114825543.

13. PWC, *The World in 2050: Will the Shift in Global Economic Power Continue?* PricewaterhouseCoopers LLP, 2015, www.pwc.com/gx/en/issues/the-economy/ assets/world-in-2050-february-2015.pdf.

14. Jeffrey Towson and Jonathan Woetzel, *The One Hour China Book: Two Peking University Professors Explain All of China Business in Six Short Stories* (Jeffrey Towson, 2014).

15. Kevin N. Laland and Bennett G. Galef, eds., *The Question of Animal Culture* (Cambridge, MA: Harvard University Press, 2009).

16. Beth Skwarecki, "Babies Learn to Recognize Words in the Womb," *Science*, August 26, 2013, accessed July 9, 2016, www.sciencemag.org/news/2013/08/babies-learn-recognize-words-womb; Jean-Pierre Lecanuet and Benoist Schaal, "Sensory Performances in the Human Foetus: A Brief Summary of Research," *Intellectica* 1, no. 34 (2002): 29–56, accessed July 9, 2016, http://intellectica.org/SiteArchives/ archives/n34/34_2_Lecanuet.pdf.

CHAPTER 1. CULTURAL AWAKENINGS

1. Lana Berkowitz, "Bush, Prince Showed Respect by Holding Hands," *Houston Chronicle*, April 27, 2005.

2. Jaime Holguin, "Abdullah-Bush Stroll Strikes Nerves," *CBS Evening News*, April 27, 2005.

3. Donald E. Brown, *Human Universals* (New York: McGraw-Hill Higher Education, 1991).

4. Andrew Keh, "And the Rio Crowd Goes Crazy! For Whatever!" *New York Times*, August 8, 2016, www.nytimes.com/2016/08/09/sports/olympics/brazilians-give-even-table-tennis-a-raucous-atmosphere.html?_r=0.

5. Associated Press, "Boisterous Brazilian Fans Rewrite Rules of Olympic Etiquette," *Denver Post*, August 11, 2016, www.denverpost.com/2016/08/11/brazilian-fans-olympic-etiquette/.

6. Robert N. St. Clair, "The Social and Cultural Construction of Silence," *International Association for Intercultural Communication* 12, no. 3 (2003).

7. Oyinkan Medubi, "A Cross-Cultural Study of Silence in Nigeria—An Ethnolinguistic Approach," University of Ilorin, Nigeria, October 29, 2009.

8. Harris Gardiner, "Where Streets Are Thronged with Strays Baring Fangs," *New York Times*, August 6, 2012; Keno Verseck, "Dog Attacks: Romania to Put Down Thousands of Strays," Spiegel Online International, September 13, 2013.

9. A. Mack and I. Rock, *Inattentional Blindness* (Cambridge, MA: MIT Press, 1998).

10. David Hambling, "Questioning Perceptual Blindness: I See No Ships," *Fortean Times*, February 2007.

11. Randall Stross, *The Wizard of Menlo Park: How Thomas Alva Edison Invented the Whole World* (New York: Three Rivers Press, 2007).

12. Terry Gross, "Habits: How They Form and How to Break Them" (interview with Charles Duhigg), *Fresh Air*, NPR, March 5, 2012.

13. Beth Azar, "Your Brain on Culture," *American Psychological Association* 41, no. 10 (November 2010).

14. Michael Blanding, "A Burgeoning Science Explores the Deep Imprint of Culture," *Tufts Magazine*, Winter 2010.

15. Joan Y. Chiao and Katherine D. Blizinsky, "Culture-Gene Coevolution of Individualism-Collectivism and the Serotonin Transporter Gene," Proceedings of the Royal Society: Biological Sciences, October 2009.

16. Charles Duhigg, *The Power of Habit: Why We Do What We Do in Life and Business* (New York: Random House, 2012).

17. Malcolm Gladwell, *Outliers: The Story of Success* (Boston, MA: Little, Brown and Company, 2008).

18. Blanding, "A Burgeoning Science Explores the Deep Imprint of Culture."

19. Geert H. Hofstede, *Culture's Consequences: Comparing Values, Behaviors, Institutions, and Organizations Across Nations*, 2nd ed. (Thousand Oaks, CA: Sage Publications, 2001).

CHAPTER 2. ME OR WE

1. Geisler Young, "2002 All-Star Game," 2000, accessed July 9, 2016, www.baseball-almanac.com/asgbox/yr2002as.shtml.

2. Jim Caple, "Ties," July 29, 2009, accessed July 9, 2016, http://sports.espn.go.com/espn/page2/story?page=caple/ties/090729

3. As a result of this game, baseball rules were officially changed—and now the league winner of the game gets home field advantage during the World Series.

4. Except in play-off games, where a winner must be determined.

5. Robert Whiting, *The Meaning of Ichiro: The New Wave from Japan and the Transformation of Our National Pastime* (United States: Hachette Book Group, 2004) (author interview November 7, 2002).

6. Kashmira Gander, "World Cup 2014: Japanese Fans Clean Stadium After Losing 2-1 to Ivory Coast," *Independent–International*, June 16, 2014, www.independent .co.uk/sport/football/international/world-cup-2014-japanese-fans-clean-stadium-after-losing-21-against-ivory-coast-9539793.html.

7. Dina Gerdeman, "How to Demotivate Your Best Employees," *Forbes*, April 8, 2013, www.forbes.com/sites/hbsworkingknowledge/2013/04/08/how-to-demotivate-your-best-employees/#10f198f65469.

8. Timothy Gubler, Ian Larkin, and Lamar Pierce, "The Dirty Laundry of Employee Award Programs: Evidence from the Field," March 4, 2013, accessed July 9, 2016, http://hbswk.hbs.edu/item/the-dirty-laundry-of-employee-award-programs-evidence-from-the-field.

9. There are plenty of ME cultures that also discourage bragging, which may be driven more by the desire to uphold a sense of equality as opposed to maintaining group harmony.

10. Nicholas Kristof, "The Japanese Could Teach Us a Thing or Two," *New York Times*, March 19, 2011, www.nytimes.com/2011/03/20/opinion/20kristof.html?_r=0.

11. H. Zhang, "Culture and Apology: The Hainan Island Incident," *World Englishes* 20 (2001): 383–391, doi: 10.1111/1467-971X.00222. Note: In fact, the United States was in Chinese airspace, and clearly should not have been.

12. Lina Yoon, *South Korea's Suicide Problem*. (Associated Press/Ahn Young-joon), July 21, 2010, www.wsj.com/articles/ SB10001424052748704684604575382213752379230; OCED.org, "Health Status–Suicide Rates–OECD Data," 2015, accessed July 9, 2016, https://data.oecd.org/ healthstat/suicide-rates.htm; *Korea's Increase in Suicides and Psychiatric Bed Numbers Is Worrying*, n.p, OCED.org, 2013, www.oecd.org/els/health-systems/ MMHC-Country-Press-Note-Korea.pdf.

13. Cornell University, "Asian American Student Suicide Rate at MIT Is Quadruple the National Average," May 2015, accessed July 9, 2016, http://reappropriate.co/2015/05/ asian-american-student-suicide-rate-at-mit-is-quadruple-the-national-average/.

14. Harumi Ozawa, "Author of Japanese Suicide Manual Has No Regrets," July 13, 2006, accessed July 9, 2016, http://mg.co.za/article/2006-07-13-author-of-japanese-suicide-manual-has-no-regrets.

15. *Wikipedia*. Wikimedia Foundation, 2016. s.v "The complete manual of suicide," accessed July 9, 2016, https://en.wikipedia.org/wiki/The_Complete_Manual_of_Suicide.

16. Nekane Basabe, and Maria Ros, "Cultural Dimensions and Social Behavior Correlates: Individualism-Collectivism and Power Distance," *Revue Internationale de Psychologie Sociale* no. 1 (2005).

17. Harry C. Triandis, *Individualism and Collectivism* (Boulder: Westview Press, 1995); Harry C. Triandis, "The Self and Social Behavior in Differing Cultural Contexts," *Psychological Review* 96, no. 3 (1989): 506–20, doi:10.1037/0033-295x.96.3.506.

18. J. Y. Chiao and K. D. Blizinsky, "Culture–Gene Coevolution of Individualism–Collectivism and the Serotonin Transporter Gene," *Proceedings of the Royal Society B: Biological Sciences* 277, no. 1681 (2009): 529–537, doi:10.1098/rspb.2009.1650.

19. C. L. Fincher, R. Thornhill, D. R. Murray, M. Schaller, "Pathogen prevalence predicts human cross-cultural variability in individualism/collectivism," *Proceedings of the Royal Society B: Biological Sciences* 275, (2008): 1279–1285, doi:10.1098/rspb.2008.0094.

20. Betha Azar, "Your Brain on Culture." American Psychological Association. November 2014, Vol. 41, No. 10.

21. "The We/Me Culture: Marketing in Korea," 2013, accessed July 9, 2016, www.koreasociety.org/corporate/the_we/me_culture_marketing_in_korea.html; Yonsei University marketing professor Dae Ryun Chung cautions that when marketing to Koreans, companies should be aware that "Koreans tend to buy housing, cars, entertainment and liquor in order to confirm their identity as Koreans. Alternately, Koreans tend to buy goods like beer, coffee and hair coloring in order to express their individual identities. If foreign marketers can create a message that balances Koreans' impulses towards "we" and "me" they may just reap huge rewards."

CHAPTER 3. SAY WHAT?

1. George Raine, and Chronicle Staff Writer, "Lost in the Translation / Milk Board Does Without Its Famous Slogan When It Woos a Latino Audience," August 25, 2001, accessed July 8, 2016, www.sfgate.com/business/article/Lost-in-the-translation-Milk-board-does-without-2884230.php.

2. Ibid.

3. Edward T. Hall, *The Anthropology of Everyday Life* (United States: Bantam Doubleday Dell Publishing Group, 1993).

4. Edward T. Hall, *Beyond Culture* (New York: Knopf Doubleday Publishing Group, 1997).

5. Ibid.

CHAPTER 4. WHAT'S NOT BEING SAID

1. Chris Irvine, "Bill Gates "Disrespects" South Korean President with Casual Handshake," *Telegraph,* April 23, 2013, www.telegraph.co.uk/news/worldnews/asia/southkorea/10011847/Bill-Gates-disrespects-South-Korean-president-with-casual-handshake.html; Yoon Min-sik, "Netizens Abuzz over Gates' Handshake with President," *Korea Herald,* April 23, 2013, accessed July 8, 2016, www.koreaherald.com/view.php?ud=20130423000714.

2. Corrinne Burns, "What Does the Way You Count on Your Fingers Say about Your Brain?" *Guardian,* February 10, 2016, www.theguardian.com/science/blog/2012/jun/26/count-fingers-brain.

3. When it comes to smiles, expression researcher Jeffrey Cohn of the University of Pittsburgh notes that all humans have facial muscles used for smiling. "There's good evidence that the motor routine involved in smiling is inborn," says Cohn.

4. John Bohannon, "Facial Expression Study Has Scientists Rethinking Darwin's 'Six Emotions,'" *Huffington Post,* April 18, 2012, www.huffingtonpost.com/2012/04/18/facial-expression-culture-_n_1434175.html; Devon Maloney, "Facial Expressions Aren't as Universal as Scientists Have Thought," *Popular Science,* April 11, 2014, accessed July 8, 2016. www.popsci.com/article/science/facial-expressions-arent-universal-we-thought.

5. R. E. Jack, O. G. B. Garrod, H. Yu, R. Caldara, and P. G. Schyns, "Facial Expressions of Emotion Are Not Culturally Universal," *Proceedings of the National Academy of Sciences* 109, no. 19 (April 16, 2012): 7241–44, doi:10.1073/pnas.1200155109.

CHAPTER 5. NOW OR LATER?

1. Øyvind Dahl, *Meanings in Madagascar: Cases of Intercultural Communication.* United States: Greenwood Press, 1999.

2. Øyvind Dahl, "When the Future Comes from Behind: Malagasy and Other Time Concepts and Some Consequences for Communication," *International Journal of Intercultural Relations* 19, no. 2 (March 1995): 197–209, doi:10.1016/0147-1767(95)00004-u.

3. Ibid.

4. Ibid.

5. Ibid.

6. Timothy Ferriss, *The 4-Hour Workweek* (New York: Crown Publishers, 2007). Currently sold in thirty-six markets, the book has sold 1,800,000 copies through more than eighty-five printings in North America; it is a Triple Crown #1 Business

Bestseller (*New York Times, Wall Street Journal,* and *Business Week*); has been on the *New York Times* Business Hardcover Bestsellers list for an unbroken four years and four months, where it has appeared for more than seven years; and is a best seller in Germany.

7. Robert N. Levine, *A Geography of Time: On Tempo, Culture, and the Pace of Life* (New York: Basic Books, 2008).

8. Edward T. Hall, *The Silent Language* (New York: Bantam Doubleday Dell Publishing Group, 1973).

9. Ibid.

10. Ibid.

11. Levine, *A Geography of Time.*

12. Lawrence T. White, "Do Cultures Segment Time Differently?" *Psychology Today,* January 27, 2012, accessed July 8, 2016, www.psychologytoday.com/blog/culture-conscious/201201/do-cultures-segment-time-differently.

13. "Train Running Late? Get a Train Delay Certificate (chien Shoumei)!" November 19, 2013, www.realestate-tokyo.com/news/train-delay-certificate/; "Sorry for the One Minute Delay: Why Tokyo's Trains Rule," September 25, 2013, accessed July 11, 2016, www.traveller.com.au/sorry-for-the-one-minute-delay-why-tokyos-trains-rule-2udv1.

14. Thomas Lafarge, Lise Martin, and Laure Gnagbé Blédou, "Voyage Entre les Lignes," August 2005, accessed July 11, 2016, http://web.archive.org/web/20080725085355/http://parisobs.nouvelobs.com/article/transports/ile-de-france/voyage-entre-les-lignes,3050,page1.html.

15. Jason Karaian, "The Swiss Are Scandalized by Trains That Run Three Minutes Behind Schedule," *Quartz,* January 13, 2014, http://qz.com/166186/the-swiss-are-scandalized-by-trains-that-run-three-minutes-behind-schedule/.

16. Nicholas Kulish, "Germany's Sense of Order vs. America's Bold Plans for the Economy," Week in Review, *New York Times,* November 16, 2014, www.nytimes.com/2009/04/05/weekinreview/05KULISH.html?_r=0.

17. Levine, *A Geography of Time.*

18. D'Vera Cohn and Andrea Caumont, "10 Demographic Trends That Are Shaping the U.S. and the World," Pew Research Center, March 31, 2016, www.pewresearch.org/fact-tank/2016/03/31/10-demographic-trends-that-are-shaping-the-u-s-and-the-world/.

19. Hope Yen, "Census: White Majority in U.S. Gone by 2043," *NBC News,* June 13, 2013, accessed July 9, 2016, http://usnews.nbcnews.com/_news/2013/06/13/18934111-census-white-majority-in-us-gone-by-2043.

20. "Autoists Do Banking from Their Car," *Popular Mechanics*, July 1930, p. 13.

21. "History: The Birth of Convenience Retailing," 7-Eleven Corporate, accessed July 9, 2016, http://corp.7-eleven.com/corp/history.

CHAPTER 6. RESPECT, RANK, AND RITUAL

1. Geert H. Hofstede, *Culture's Consequences: Comparing Values, Behaviors, Institutions, and Organizations Across Nations*, 2nd ed. (Thousand Oaks, CA: Sage Publications, 2001).

2. BBC, "Guayabera Shirt Now Official Cuban Formal Dress Code," *BBC*, October 7, 2010, www.bbc.com/news/11492327.

3. Sean Upton-McLaughlin, "Chinese Dining Etiquette," China Culture Corner, August 1, 2013, accessed July 9, 2016, https://chinaculturecorner.com/2013/08/01/dining-etiquette-in-china/.

4. John Leland, "Cultural Differences," At War (blog), *New York Times*, December 5, 2009, http://atwar.blogs.nytimes.com/2009/12/04/cultural-differences/.

5. John Spacey, "How to Pour a Drink in Japan," Japan Talk, 2002, accessed July 9, 2016, www.japan-talk.com/jt/new/how-to-pour-a-drink-in-Japan.

6. Michael Landers, "Culture Crossing," 2014, http://guide.culturecrossing.net/basics_business_student_details.php?Id=16&CID=105.

7. Lee Marshall, "Ordering Coffee in Italy: The 10 Commandments," *Telegraph*, April 26, 2016, www.telegraph.co.uk/travel/destinations/europe/italy/articles/italian-coffee-culture-a-guide/.

8. Barbara Kiviat, "The Big Gulp at Starbucks," *Time*, December 10, 2006, accessed July 9, 2016, http://content.time.com/time/magazine/article/0,9171,1568488,00.html.

9. Entrepreneur Media, "Howard Schultz," *Entrepreneur*, October 10, 2008, accessed July 9, 2016, www.entrepreneur.com/article/197692.

10. Eric Schlosser, "Americans Are Obsessed with Fast Food: The Dark Side of the All-American Meal," *CBS News*, accessed April 14, 2014, www.cbsnews.com/news/americans-are-obsessed-with-fast-food-the-dark-side-of-the-all-american-meal/.

11. Placed, "White Paper: Dining out in America Part 1: The Quick Service Restaurant Landscape," Placed Insights, n.d., accessed July 9, 2016, www.placed.com/resources/white-papers/quick-service-restaurant-landscape.

12. Randy James, "A Brief History of McDonald's Abroad," *Time*, October 28, 2009, accessed July 9, 2016, http://content.time.com/time/world/article/0,8599,1932839,00.html.

13. Lucy Fancourt, Bredesen Lewis, and Nicholas Madjka, "Born in the USA, Made in France: How McDonald's Succeeds in the Land of Michelin Stars," Knowledge@

Wharton, Wharton School, University of Pennsylvania, January 3, 2012, accessed July 9, 2016, http://knowledge.wharton.upenn.edu/article/born-in-the-usa-made-in-france-how-mcdonalds-succeeds-in-the-land-of-michelin-stars/; Eleanor Beardsley, "Why McDonald's in France Doesn't Feel Like Fast Food," NPR, January 24, 2012, accessed July 9, 2016, www.npr.org/sections/thesalt/2012/01/24/145698222/why-mcdonalds-in-france-doesnt-feel-like-fast-food.

14. Sun Kim, "In France, McDonald's Refreshes Its Brand with Architecture and Design," ZDNet, November 21, 2011, accessed July 9, 2016, www.zdnet.com/article/in-france-mcdonalds-refreshes-its-brand-with-architecture-and-design/.

CHAPTER 7. CORE VALUES

1. David C. Pollock and Ruth E. Van Reken, *Third Culture Kids: The Experience of Growing Up Among Worlds* (Yarmouth, ME, and London: Nicholas Brealey Publishing, 2001); Andrea M. Moore and Gina G. Barker, "Confused or Multicultural: Third Culture Individuals' Cultural Identity," *International Journal of Intercultural Relations* 36, no. 4 (July 2012): 553–62, doi:10.1016/j.ijintrel.2011.11.002.

2. Ivan Simonovic, "Statement by Assistant Secretary-General for Human Rights, Ivan Simonovic at the Side-Event on the Margins of the 69th Session of the UN General Assembly on Launch of OHCHR's Recommended Principles and Guidelines on Human Rights at International Borders," October 23, 2014, accessed July 10, 2016, www.ohchr.org/EN/NewsEvents/Pages/DisplayNews.aspx?NewsID=15252&LangID=E.

3. L. Robert Kohls, *Values Americans Live By* (Washington, DC: The Washington International Center, 1984).

4. Ibid.

5. Ibid.

6. Sean Poulter and Mark Duell, "Tesco Announces 'Horror Show' £6.38bn Loss -Biggest in 97-Year History," *Daily Mail*, April 24, 2015, www.dailymail.co.uk/news/article-3049662/Tesco-set-announce-horror-5bn-loss-Retailer-downturn-one-biggest-British-history-seismic-shift-shopping-habits.html.

7. Brad Tuttle, "Tale of Two Supermarkets: Why Fresh & Easy Flopped and Fairway Flies High," *Time*, April 18, 2013, accessed July 10, 2016, http://business.time.com/2013/04/18/tale-of-two-supermarkets-why-fresh-easy-flopped-and-fairway-flies-high/.

8. Ibid.

9. "Five Years In, Fresh & Easy Markets Are a Flop," *Los Angeles Times,* March 21, 2013, accessed July 10, 2016. http://articles.latimes.com/2013/mar/21/business/la-fi-fresh-easy-woes-20130321.

10. Tuttle, "Tale of Two Supermarkets."

11. Ibid.

12. Lynne Bateson, "Why Tesco's Fresh & Easy Turned Americans Off," *Guardian*, December 5, 2012, www.theguardian.com/business/2012/dec/05/tesco-fresh-easy-turned-americans-off.

13. Poulter and Duell, "Tesco Announces 'Horror Show.'"

14. Clotaire Rapaille, *The Culture Code: An Ingenious Way to Understand Why People Around the World Buy and Live as They Do* (New York: Broadway Books, 2006).

15. Ibid.

16. Ibid.

17. Ibid.

18. Linda Tischler, "Ideo's David Kelley on 'Design Thinking,'" *Co.Design*, April 12, 2016, www.fastcodesign.com/1139331/ideos-david-kelley-design-thinking.

19. Tim Brown, "The 7 Values That Drive IDEO," Design Thinking: Thoughts by Tim Brown, January 21, 2014, accessed July 10, 2016, http://designthinking.ideo.com/?p=1282.

20. Ibid.

21. Although cofounder Eduardo Saverin was born in Brazil, he emigrated to the United States when he was just eleven years old.

22. David Kirkpatrick, *The Facebook Effect: The Inside Story of the Company That Is Connecting the World* (New York: Simon & Schuster Adult Publishing Group, 2010).

23. Alice Kirkland, "10 Countries Where Facebook Has Been Banned," Index, February 4, 2014, accessed July 10, 2016, www.indexoncensorship.org/2014/02/10-countries-facebook-banned/.

CONCLUSION: CULTURE CROSSINGS PAST, PRESENT, AND FUTURE

1. Greg Toppo and Paul Overberg, "Second Immigration Wave Lifts Diversity to Record High: Collision of Cultures, Languages and Politics Poses Perils and Promises." "The Changing Face of America: 100 Years of Diversity. Gathering Places. 'Library Is the Living Room' of a New Jersey Town," *USA Today*, n.d., www.usatoday.com/story/news/nation/2014/10/21/diversity-race-ethnicity-change-100-years/16211133/.

2. Ashley Kirk, "Mapped: Which Country Has the Most Immigrants?" *Telegraph*, January 21, 2016, www.telegraph.co.uk/news/worldnews/middleeast/12111108/Mapped-Which-country-has-the-most-immigrants.html.

BIBLIOGRAPHY

Axtell, Roger E. *Gestures: The Do's and Taboos of Body Language Around the World.* New York: Wiley, 1997.

Conditions. "Language Translation from #1 UK Online Translation Agency." 2016. Accessed July 1, 2016. www.kwintessential.co.uk/.

Culture Crossing. "Country Guides to Culture, Etiquette, Customs & More!" 2014. Accessed July 1, 2016. http://guide.culturecrossing.net/.

Hall, Edward T. *The Hidden Dimension.* New York: Bantam Doubleday Dell Publishing Group, 1988.

———. *The Silent Language.* New York: Bantam Doubleday Dell Publishing Group, 1973.

———. *Beyond Culture.* New York: Knopf Doubleday Publishing Group, 1997.

Hofstede, Geert H. *Culture's Consequences: Comparing Values, Behaviors, Institutions, and Organizations Across Nations,* 2nd ed. Thousand Oaks, CA: Sage Publications, 2001.

Kohls, Robert L. *Survival Kit for Overseas Living.* n.p.: Intercultural Press, 1984.

Lee, Charles. *Cowboys and Dragons: Shattering Cultural Myths to Advance Chinese-American Business Relations.* United States: Kaplan, 2003.

Levine, Robert N. *A Geography of Time: On Tempo, Culture, and the Pace of Life.* United States: Basic Books, 2008.

Lewis, Richard D. *When Cultures Collide: Leading Across Cultures,* 3rd ed. Boston: Nicholas Brealey International, 2005.

Meyer, Erin. *The Culture Map: Breaking Through the Invisible Boundaries of Global Business.* United States: The Perseus Books Group, 2014.

Molinsky, Andy. *Global Dexterity: How to Adapt Your Behavior Across Cultures Without Losing Yourself in the Process.* Boston, MA: Harvard Business Review Press, 2012.

Williams, Jeremy. *Don't They Know It's Friday? Cross-Cultural Considerations for Business and Life in the Gulf.* Dubai: Motivate Publishing, 1999.

Rapaille, Clotaire. *The Culture Code: An Ingenious Way to Understand Why People Around the World Buy and Live as They Do.* New York: Broadway Books, 2006.

Schmitz, Joerg. *Cultural Orientations Guide: The Roadmap to Cultural Competence,* 5th ed. Princeton, NJ: Princeton Training Press, 2006.

Storti, Craig. *Figuring Foreigners Out: A Practical Guide,* 3rd ed. United Kingdom: Intercultural Press, 2000.

Towson, Jeffrey, and Jonathan Woetzel. *The One Hour China Book: Two Peking*

University Professors Explain All of China Business in Six Short Stories. Cayman Islands: Towson Group, 2014.

Trompenaars, Fons, and Charles Hampden-Turner. *Riding the Waves Culture: Understanding Cultural Diversity in Business.* United Kingdom: Nicholas Brealey Publishing, 2000.

Whiting, Robert. *The Chrysanthemum and the Bat: The Game Japanese Play.* n.p.: Permanent Press, 1977.

———. *The Meaning of Ichiro: The New Wave from Japan and the Transformation of Our National Pastime.* United States: Hachette Book Group, 2004.

———. *You Gotta Have Wa.* New York: Knopf Doubleday Publishing Group, 2009.

| ACKNOWLEDGMENTS

To my parents, Marcia and Lester Landers, whose courage and cultural curiosity led them to move our family to Colombia, Brazil, and the Dominican Republic. I can't thank you enough for giving me a unique experience that truly shaped my life and my work. To my sisters, Carole and Jennifer, for joining me on our shared cross-cultural journey and supporting me with love and guidance.

To my professors and classmates from Lesley University—Dr. L. Robert Kohls, Dr. Zareen Karani Araoz, Dr. Sylvia Cowan, and Dr. Jay Jones—I thank you for opening my mind and laying a solid foundation from which I have been able to grow my career in the field.

I would like to thank the whole team at Berrett-Koehler, including Jeevan and Anna, for believing in the message and enabling and supporting me to publish this book.

Big thanks to Rebecca Gradinger and the team and Fletcher & Company for all the support and effort in finding the book a home.

I offer my deep gratitude to the many people who helped me with this book: to those who provided support, talked things over, wrote, read, offered comments, and allowed me to quote their remarks. In particular, Tamara Moan, Paisley Gregg, Melanie Sperling, Diana Bufalini, Harris and Irene Grossman, and Marcia and Lester Landers.

To my wife, Lisa Landers: without you this book would not have been written. From the time we met thirteen years ago, you have been enthusiastically and wholeheartedly supporting my career. You have willingly sacrificed your time and sometimes your career over the years to allow me to travel the globe doing my work. Seven years ago we first hatched the idea for this book, and you have been my partner in helping it take shape ever since. As it has become more and more of a reality, you have shown undying patience, understanding, compassion, and fortitude in situations that have been trying at times. Your unique ability to help me craft the thoughts and messages I wanted to convey in a way that people could really hear them has proved invaluable. This book is a joint production. It is yours just as much as mine. *Te amo con todo mi corazon!*

Hugs, kisses, and many thanks to my daughter, Talia, whose support, patience, and excitement for the book have been essential. I'm grateful that you share our passion for exploring new cultures and places, and I hope you will feel proud to see this book on the shelves of the bookstores we frequent. I love you!

Last but not least, I need to thank those who have had an impact on me over the course of the years: from all the friends and teachers at CNG, EARJ, and CMS to colleagues and friends during my time in Japan and other places around the world.

INDEX

Abdullah, Crown Prince, 12–13
acceptable behaviors. *See* disrespectful behaviors (perceived)
Adult Third Culture Kids (ATCKs), 151
advertising. *See* marketing/advertising
African cultures, touch/touching, 103
aggressive communication styles, 71–77
alcoholic drinks etiquette, 144–145
Ambady, Nalini, 33
American culture. *See* United States culture
animals, treatment of, 27–28
anthropology, cultural, 34
anxiety, 61
apologies, 46
Arab cultures, 21–22, 52, 95, 103, 104, 117
arrival time. *See* time perception
assertive communication styles, 71–77
assumptions, 43, 55–56, 75
ATCKs (Adult Third Culture Kids), 151
attitude, 34–36
axioms, 164–165. *See also* proverbs and sayings

baggage, cultural, 18–19
baseball games, reactions to, 40–41
beckoning (come here) gesture, 94–95, 107
behaviors
adjusting your, 136–137
assessment of, 16–17
beliefs and values affecting our, 18–19
as clues, 58

core values as dictators of, 153
of direct and indirect communicators, 70–71
disrespectful/acceptable (*See* disrespectful behaviors (perceived))
formal/informal, 130–131
frames of reference for understanding, 29
frustration with other cultures', 153–154
genetic factors in, 61
as indicators of core values, 170
influence of Me-We ideologies on, 43
during interviews, 43
invisible elements of, 15–16
mirroring, 149
misinterpreting, 55–56
modifying, 112
organizational, 35–36
others' views of American's, 154–156
patterns of, 162–163
perceptions of, 72–73
understanding reasons for, 14–15
See also gestures
beliefs, 18–19, 24, 28–29, 57–58
Bharucha, Jamshed, 32
biases, 43, 77, 105
Blizinsky, Katherine, 60–61
body language. *See* nonverbal communication
bowing when greeting others, 104–105
brain, cultural shaping of, 31–33
Brannen, Chris, 78
Brannen Group, 78
Brazilian culture, 22–23, 92–93, 100–101, 123
Brown, Tim, 164
Buddhism, 83

bus boarding, 13–15
Bush, George W., 12–13
business cards, 142, 143–144, 149
business transactions, 172

California, cultural differences in, 65
Canadian culture, 60, 101–103
ceremonies, 143, 145–147
Chiao, Joan, 32, 60–61
China/Chinese culture, 20–21, 26, 46, 51–52, 51–53, 95, 115
Christianity, 83
clothing/dress codes, 129, 133, 134, 149
codes/coding, 34, 159–160
coffee etiquette, 145–147
cognitive functions, 31–32
collectivist instincts, 32
college towns, proportion of foreign born students in, 3
Colombian culture, 93, 101, 111–112, 138–139
Colombo, Sri Lanka, 13–15
communication crashes, 69–70, 76–77
communication styles
American, 154–155
comfort with silence, 81–85
context and, 68–70
by country, 77–80
dealing with silence, 84–85
eye contact during, 104
generalizations, 36–37
groups' development of, 80
importance of effective, 172–173
misinterpreting, 2
perceiving and reacting to different, 71–77
personal preferences in styles of, 67–71
preferences, 78

Michael Landers is the founder and president of Culture Crossing, Inc., a global consulting company dedicated to finding innovative solutions for groups and individuals working in challenging global contexts.

Over the past twenty years, Michael has designed and facilitated programs for global executives and managers with whom he works to build essential skills in arenas such as leadership and coaching, cross-cultural communication and team building, cultural diversity and inclusion, sustained employee engagement, and international sales and negotiations.

Michael has conducted business in over thirty countries, which has given him a strong understanding of the pitfalls and challenges business professionals often face while working with the global community. Although he was born in the United States, Michael was raised in countries throughout Latin America. He returned to the United States to receive a bachelor's degree in international business, followed by a master's degree in cross-cultural studies from Lesley College. Michael's language skills—he is fluent in Spanish and Brazilian Portuguese and proficient in Japanese and Italian—enable him to establish strong and sustained connections with many of his clients. He also shares his expertise with others through lectures and speaking engagements at schools, universities, and other institutions around the globe.

Culture Crossing's clients include Apple, Google, Samsung, HSBC, SAP, Novartis, Fiat Worldwide, Isuzu Motors of Japan, Airbnb, Kaiser Permanente, Cal Atlantic Homes, and Mead Johnson, among others.

Berrett–Koehler
Publishers

Berrett-Koehler is an independent publisher dedicated to an ambitious mission: Connecting people and ideas to create a world that works for all.

We believe that the solutions to the world's problems will come from all of us, working at all levels: in our organizations, in our society, and in our own lives. Our BK Business books help people make their organizations more humane, democratic, diverse, and effective (we don't think there's any contradiction there). Our BK Currents books offer pathways to creating a more just, equitable, and sustainable society. Our BK Life books help people create positive change in their lives and align their personal practices with their aspirations for a better world.

All of our books are designed to bring people seeking positive change together around the ideas that empower them to see and shape the world in a new way.

And we strive to practice what we preach. At the core of our approach is Stewardship, a deep sense of responsibility to administer the company for the benefit of all of our stakeholder groups including authors, customers, employees, investors, service providers, and the communities and environment around us. Everything we do is built around this and our other key values of quality, partnership, inclusion, and sustainability.

This is why we are both a B-Corporation and a California Benefit Corporation—a certification and a for-profit legal status that require us to adhere to the highest standards for corporate, social, and environmental performance.

We are grateful to our readers, authors, and other friends of the company who consider themselves to be part of the BK Community. We hope that you, too, will join us in our mission.

A BK Business Book

We hope you enjoy this BK Business book. BK Business books pioneer new leadership and management practices and socially responsible approaches to business. They are designed to provide you with groundbreaking and practical tools to transform your work and organizations while upholding the triple bottom line of people, planet, and profits. High-five!

To find out more, visit **www.bkconnection.com**.

Berrett–Koehler
Publishers

Connecting people and ideas
to create a world that works for all

Dear Reader,

Thank you for picking up this book and joining our worldwide community of Berrett-Koehler readers. We share ideas that bring positive change into people's lives, organizations, and society.

To welcome you, we'd like to offer you a free e-book. You can pick from among twelve of our bestselling books by entering the promotional code **BKP92E** here: http://www.bkconnection.com/welcome.

When you claim your free e-book, we'll also send you a copy of our e-news-letter, the *BK Communiqué*. Although you're free to unsubscribe, there are many benefits to sticking around. In every issue of our newsletter you'll find

- A free e-book
- Tips from famous authors
- Discounts on spotlight titles
- Hilarious insider publishing news
- A chance to win a prize for answering a riddle

Best of all, our readers tell us, "Your newsletter is the only one I actually read." So claim your gift today, and please stay in touch!

Sincerely,

Charlotte Ashlock
Steward of the BK Website

Questions? Comments? Contact me at bkcommunity@bkpub.com.

MIX
Paper from
responsible sources
FSC® C016245

Certified

Corporation
bcorporation.net